Leap of Faith

Leap of Faith

Finding Love the Modern Way

CAMERON HAMILTON
& LAUREN SPEED

G

GALLERY BOOKS

NEW YORK   LONDON   TORONTO   SYDNEY   NEW DELHI

G

Gallery Books
An Imprint of Simon & Schuster, Inc.
1230 Avenue of the Americas
New York, NY 10020

First Gallery Books hardcover edition June 2021

GALLERY BOOKS and colophon are registered
trademarks of Simon & Schuster, Inc.

For information about special discounts for bulk purchases,
please contact Simon & Schuster Special Sales at 1-866-506-1949
or business@simonandschuster.com.

The Simon & Schuster Speakers Bureau can bring authors to
your live event. For more information or to book an event, contact the
Simon & Schuster Speakers Bureau at 1-866-248-3049 or
visit our website at www.simonspeakers.com.

Interior design by Michelle Marchese

Manufactured in the United States of America

1   3   5   7   9   10   8   6   4   2

Library of Congress Cataloging-in-Publication Data

Names: Hamilton, Cameron (Cameron Reid), author. | Speed, Lauren, author.
Title: Leap of faith / Cameron Hamilton & Lauren Speed.
Description: First Gallery Books hardcover edition. | New York : Gallery
Books, 2021. | Summary: "The fan-favorite couple from Netflix's Love Is
Blind share their ups and downs after two years of marriage, love advice
for the modern world, and behind-the-scenes anecdotes from the pods"—
Provided by publisher.
Identifiers: LCCN 2020055310 (print) | LCCN 2020055311 (ebook) | ISBN
9781982167134 (hardcover) | ISBN 9781982167141 (trade paperback) | ISBN
9781982167158 (ebook)
Subjects: LCSH: Hamilton, Cameron (Cameron Reid) | Speed, Lauren. | Love is
blind (Television program) | Television personalities—United
States—Biography. | Dating shows (Television programs)—United States.
| Interracial marriage. | Man-woman relationships. | Husband and wife.
Classification: LCC PN1992.4.A2 H36 2021 (print) | LCC PN1992.4.A2
(ebook) | DDC 791.45/6--dc23
LC record available at https://lccn.loc.gov/2020055310
LC ebook record available at https://lccn.loc.gov/2020055311

ISBN 978-1-9821-6713-4
ISBN 978-1-9821-6715-8 (ebook)

*We dedicate this book to both Pams and Bills (our parents)
for being our first loves.*

contents

CONTENTS

Part III

preface

NOVEMBER 2020, ATLANTA

The day had finally arrived. The party was about to begin and we still couldn't say whether we were more excited or nervous for what was going to unfold. The past couple weeks had been hectic. We'd been shooting almost nonstop for a "where are they now?" follow-up series to *Love Is Blind*. As part of the big finale, the producers asked if they could plan and film a two-year joint wedding anniversary party with Amber and Barnett. Of course, that meant production also taking over the planning and preparation of the celebration. Which is how we found ourselves looking out across downtown Atlanta from the glass elevator we were taking up to Ventanas—the rooftop venue where guests were already starting to gather.

We spent most of the day at home, appreciating some time just the two of us, getting ready, and reminiscing about our journey together. Had it really been two years since *Love Is Blind* had turned us from strangers into Mr. and Mrs. Cameron and Lauren

Hamilton in the span of seven weeks? Time had flown by, but we had grown so much over the course of our short marriage, both as a couple and as individuals. We had over a year to ourselves to build our marriage and process the experience of *Love Is Blind* in private before being launched into the public eye with the Netflix premiere in February 2020. Since then, we have been figuring out how best to manage the newfound opportunities and attention, while also moving forward from the show.

It was both rewarding and taxing to be back in front of the cameras, as we once again opened ourselves up to being completely vulnerable. The difference this time around was that we'd been married for two years; there was no uncertainty about whether we would say "I do" at the altar. Though we've gotten used to sharing our relationship and our lives with the world, it will always be an energy exchange. It's not easy to talk about subjects as intimate as how our relationship has been developing, what we've been working on, and the challenges we have yet to overcome. But we are happy to share our story because of all the people around the world who support us and send us their love. So many people have reached out to tell us that our story has inspired them not to give up hope on love. Those are the people we continue sharing our lives for. At the end of the day, we wouldn't want to be doing anything else.

We reminded ourselves of all this as we made our way to the party. We also wondered what the night would hold. Nearly everyone from the original cast had been invited to the party. Would Mark show up, given that he was now engaged with a baby on the way? How were things with Gi and Damian? How would the rest of the cast respond to us, plus Amber and Barnett? Would people be happy for us or upset that the night was focused on our marriage? We came to the mutual agreement that we weren't going to worry about anyone else but the two of us—this was our anniversary after all. Regardless of what was going on with the rest of the cast, we were going to make this night about celebrating the gift the last two years had been and appreciating each other for what we have brought into each other's lives.

And hey, this was still our big night, right? So you know we had to make an entrance! Lauren dazzled in her two-piece purple dress with the serpentine train she nicknamed Veronica. And Cameron donned his peacock green custom-tailored suit by the designer Don Morphy. We wouldn't want anyone to forget whose party this was, would we?

We were fairly certain that the night would have its fair share of drama. After all, this was the first time that the "pod squad," as we used to call ourselves on set, would be together as a group since shooting the reunion episode. We knew the night could turn on a dime with all of us gathered together. The mood could be fun and relaxed one minute, then all hell could break loose the next.

We had done our best to steer clear of the drama on *Love Is Blind*, and that was our mindset going into the anniversary party too. It wasn't that we were bothered by drama; we simply felt out of place in it. The reality is that *Love Is Blind* was an intense, life-changing experience that is not to be taken lightly. While the show's many zany moments were amusing, it can be easy to lose sight of the fact that this experience was challenging for everyone and has left a lasting impact. While we may not always see eye-to-eye with other members of the cast, we will always feel a special bond with them, having been through the experiment together. And *Love Is Blind* will always be an important milestone in our lives.

So, did the night have fireworks as expected? You'll have to watch the episode on Netflix to find out. All we can tell you is that it will not disappoint! In the end, though, the party for us was another reminder that we have our own story to tell—and that it's still just beginning.

That takes us to *Leap of Faith*. This book is the story of how we came to find ourselves on *Love Is Blind*, the many parts that didn't make it to the screen, and the journey we've been on together since saying our "I dos." It's also our chance to share the secrets behind how we were able to find love the way we did and how we have kept our marriage growing through many trials and tribulations. We realize that a couple years of happy marriage doesn't make us authorities on the subject. But the unique circumstances of our union, especially the incredible leap of faith it required, have given us special insights that we think can help others find their own deep and lasting connection. If nothing else, we think it's a one-of-a-kind love story. We're so happy to share it with you.

Leap of Faith

Part 1

chapter one

A NOT-SO-MODEL LIFE

Lauren

I always figured that by the time I turned thirty I'd have it all figured out. The amazing career, the handsome hubby, the beautiful home, maybe a baby on my hip and another on the way. But my thirtieth birthday had come and gone and these things never felt farther away. By the summer of 2017, a year before *Love Is Blind* even crossed my radar, I was in a drought season praying for rain. Those were some humbling, character-building times in my life.

For as long as I could remember, I'd been the person people came to when *they* were down and out. Trouble in paradise? Talk to Lauren. Issues at work? Go tell Lauren. I was proud of the fact that people saw me as strong and dependable. That's even more reason why 2017 was such a tough year for me. It was one of the toughest years of my life.

Besides being people's go-to, I've always been a go-getter, a trait I share with my dad. He worked his tail off for decades as an editor, writer, and producer notably working with BET (Black Entertainment Television) among other publications, networks, and game changers in the industry. "You want to get ahead in this world," he'd say to me and my older brother, Nick, "you gotta work hard and smart." In high school, while most of my peers were still experimenting with hair and makeup, I was glamming it up in pageants and working as a model.

By the age of nineteen, I was working with industry agents and gaining valuable experience working with some of the best photographers in the business.

I started to push for more TV and radio opportunities; modeling was fun but my personality bubbled over like hot soup boiling on a stove. But I was still building my portfolio and had to clock in more time. Patience has never really been one of my virtues. However, I kept pushing, and eventually the TV and radio spots started pouring in as well.

My twenties were more of the same, in terms of hard work and hustle. I graduated from Eastern Michigan University with a degree in film and media. I hit the ground running, spending a few years working and playing in Detroit before moving to Washington, DC, and eventually on to Atlanta, where I landed in 2015. I was doing a lot of creative jobs during this time, which was good for my mind and soul, but not so good for my bank account. Believe you me, the starving-artist routine gets old in a hurry after age twenty-five.

And so in my late twenties, I finally had to bite the bullet and take a corporate job in one of the anonymous office buildings in Atlanta, which really killed my spirit and was a blow to my creative ego. I was so out of my element. I remember retreating to the bathroom and crying on multiple occasions. *Why am I here?* I'd ask myself. *I don't belong here.* But I had to pay the bills. This went on for longer than I like to admit, close to two years.

With my thirty-first birthday fast approaching, I decided enough was enough. I scraped together my savings, gave notice with the corporate bosses, and continued my goal of growing my own company, a boutique creative marketing agency called The Speed Brand. I titled the business with the family name because I envisioned it being a true family venture. Entertainment has always been the Speed family business. At our family's encouragement, my brother and I used to film sketches as kids, using the clunky VHS camcorder that our aunt Shelia had given to him for his birthday back in the early nineties. Nick still works in music production, creating his own tracks, DJing, and promoting other artists.

One of my favorite projects with The Speed Brand to date was directing a music video for Nick, for a song called "Throw Sum" that he wrote and performed. It's a moody hip-hop beat that captures the soul and passion of our family. We shot the entire video in Detroit, our hometown, using our favorite cityscapes as backdrops. It was everything I imagined for the business.

Other projects were more bread and butter, like the Valentine's Day segment I produced for CBS Radio, going around the city asking people about their love lives. My talent was helping brands and businesses make creative statements with the right visuals and voice. I did it all—videography, content creation, storytelling, photography, you name it. I had always been involved in the arts in some shape or form, so I had built up the skills and creative confidence to take on any challenge.

Based on my early success, I expected the business to take off. I don't think I was being overly confident. I believed in myself and I also felt that I brought a unique skill set and life experience. I knew I had a story to tell and I wanted to share that story with the world.

For about six months, well into 2017, life was good. I was happy to be back in the creative space, flexing muscles that had gone soft in corporate. Unfortunately, the good times didn't last. As hard as I hustled, I was struggling to bring in enough new business to make ends meet.

I had some savings, but the money was running out fast. I was sinking. By the end of September 2017, I was more depressed than I'd ever been in my life. On most days, it took all my energy just to leave the house. The first of the month was coming—and rent was due. I'd been late the last few months. I was avoiding my landlord because I was so disappointed in myself, but finally I sent him an email explaining the situation.

"Listen, Lauren, we understand life happens," he replied. "But if you're not on time this month, we're going to have to evict you."

As hard as that conversation was, it was nothing compared to the phone calls to my mom and dad later that night. I was all out of options. I had to ask them for money. We had always been comfortable growing up—not the wealthiest family in the community, but never worried about there being enough food in the cupboard. But as an adult who considered myself pretty responsible and self-sufficient, it was more about my pride taking a hit. Fortunately, they're extremely loving and supportive.

"We understand, Lauren," my mom said. "We hate that you're having to go through this."

With the financial support from my parents, I was able to stay afloat for another few months. But I knew something had to give. I would be turning thirty-two in a couple months. Hitting thirty had been hard enough. The fact that almost two years had passed and I was treading water, at best, filled me with sadness.

I'd been turning more and more to prayer during this time. My bank account was almost down to zero, but I was still able to keep my phone on, so I'd watch sermons on the internet at night and then have these long talks with God. "I know there's a reason you're taking me through these trials," I'd say. "You must have some kind of plan for me."

I believed that in my heart. I just had no idea what the plan could be.

I can't say my prayers were answered overnight. But after that humbling moment, things started to pick up. I managed to find some temp work that paid well, helping make ends meet. Then a few more clients rolled into The Speed Brand, thanks to a major push on social media. I'd always been into IG and Snapchat for my personal life, but I started leveraging the platforms more and more to help build my business. I'd post pics of myself BTS, working on the set of a shoot with the hashtags #videographerinatl and #creativeinatl. Brands really responded. I ended up getting more music video work, a cool sneaker documentary, and all kinds of creative beauty tutorials for glam makers and fashion bloggers.

I wasn't rolling in dough all of a sudden, but I had room to breathe. I even had enough money in the bank to do some traveling. I had always wanted to get out there and see the world. And as I started to come out of this very dark episode of my life, it felt like the time was right to wander. This was what I like to call my *Eat, Pray, Love* phase, a period of deep introspection that I knew would be well served by exploring through travel and immersing myself in inspiration and new cultures. I was convinced that if I was going to get my life back on track and pointed in a positive direction, I would need to engage in some serious soul-searching. Traveling would give me the time and physical separation from my everyday life to allow this.

I spent a lot of time staring at a map of the world on my phone, trying to figure out which destination tugged at my soul the most. When I was growing up, my dad always *loved* Cuban singer Celia Cruz. He'd play her music while cooking dinner or driving my brother and me around in the car. She was the spitting image of his mom, my grandmother, whom I never got a chance to meet. "Look at these pictures," my dad would say. "They look exactly alike!"

How about Havana? I thought to myself one night. From that point forward, the trip to Cuba became like a pilgrimage in my mind. This would be my first truly international trip (not counting Canada), and the fact that I was on my own made it all the more meaningful.

Walking through the streets of Havana, with its colorful buildings, loud music, and vintage cars, was a total awakening. One night, I was out and about when I stumbled onto a lively street party. The salsa music was blaring, and everyone was dancing up a storm. This Cuban guy grabbed me and pulled me into the dance circle, in a totally sweet and innocent way. I could literally feel the depression of the last year melting away. I felt myself exhale for the first time in ages. I was truly happy and joyful because I knew I was exactly where I needed to be.

Back home in Atlanta, I kept the whole *Eat, Pray, Love* vision quest vibe going. I had found a brand-new respect for myself in Cuba and I was excited to apply it to every aspect of my life. I was living in Buckhead, a trendy, upscale neighborhood that's known as "The Beverly Hills of Atlanta." I had this incredible apartment that became such a source of pride, especially since only a few months earlier I'd been on the verge of eviction. It was small, but it was the perfect size for me and my creative projects. I built a miniature studio in the living room and made the space exactly how I wanted it. I could roll out of bed and create whatever was on my mind.

Most of my girlfriends were single, including my homegirl Tiffany, or Tiff as I call her. We were the single girls club living our best lives like a *Sex and the City* episode. Something inside me clicked. I decided if I was going to be thirty plus and single, I was going to enjoy myself, full-on Carrie Bradshaw–style. Taking life by the horns and living it to its fullest extent.

The trip to Cuba had kick-started my change in perspective, while also giving me a serious case of wanderlust. After a few months of Atlanta living, I felt the pull again. This time, I set my sights on Italy, another country steeped in culture that was high on my bucket list.

One morning there, I ventured out with my camera and came upon a street market brimming with life. Vendors were hawking all kinds of wares, from textiles to gelato. I started snapping photos. My Italian isn't very good, but it wasn't long before I heard the unmistakable sound of catcalls from the local Italian men. The signori were smitten! I'll admit, I was a little surprised at how forward they were (you don't need to be fluent to understand the language of desire!), especially since I was one of the few Black women I'd seen during my trip.

The art in Italy, meanwhile, stirred my creative spirit. Standing before the Sistine Chapel, the Roman Colosseum, or any number of Italian masterpieces, I was completely awed by the sense of history and permanence. The artwork itself was amazing, but I was equally intrigued by the artists themselves. What was on Michelangelo's mind as he sculpted *David* from a single block of marble? What was Leonardo's life like as he put his imaginings of the Last Supper to canvas? These musings made me think about my own creative efforts. Could I ever create something that would outlast my time on earth? Was there a masterpiece in me? Seeing how this great Italian art continues to inspire people lit a fire under me to want to inspire others in the same way.

Traveling the world was an intensely positive experience, but in the back of my mind I knew that it couldn't last forever. After a bumpy liftoff, my thirties were now off to an amazing start. All the work I put into myself was paying off in a big way. Where was life headed next?

That was the million-dollar question. Despite all the progress I'd made over the last year, I didn't have a good answer. I was still searching for the right rhythm and balance. I knew that the single girls club in Atlanta was no more sustainable than a jet-setting life of leisure. Where was the middle ground? What was my equilibrium?

It was right around this time, early in the summer of 2018, that a strange DM came through on my Instagram account. Something about a new dating show being filmed in Atlanta. . . .

chapter two

STUCK IN THE BORED ROOM

Cameron

"Bad news, guys," the helicopter pilot said. "You've got a black bear right above you on the cliff and he's pretty hot and bothered. We're gonna have to find you another way out."

I've always been the adventurous type—as a kid, I fantasized about life as an intrepid explorer or archaeologist, like Indiana Jones—but being surrounded by both a blazing wildfire and a frightened bear wasn't exactly what I had in mind.

It was the summer of 2012 and I was on the side of a mountain in remote Quebec, working as a wildland firefighter. When I was growing up in small-town Maine, most of my early summer jobs were pretty standard—painting buildings, mowing lawns, and taking care of the grounds at the local beach. But as soon as I turned sixteen, my father suggested I take some firefighting classes. Once I earned my "red card" firefighting certification, I spent the next eight summers in the wilderness.

Besides the adventure of the work, I was able to make a lot more money fighting fires than pushing a lawn mower or wielding a paintbrush. Plus, I was proud to be doing work that protected people's lives. Working with the Maine Forest Service, I fought many fires in my home state, but I also went up and down the East Coast battling blazes, from Florida all the way up into Canada.

That mountaintop in remote Quebec was definitely one of the hairiest situations I'd encountered on the job. We were working on a monstrous fire, about three hundred thousand acres, and it was raging fast across the Canadian range. Firefighters are taught safety protocols (always have an escape route, recognize "Watch Out" situations, et cetera), but sometimes you can't avoid the danger.

My squad had been taking helicopters to a remote part of the fire line every day for a couple weeks trying to contain the blaze. There are different strategies for this. In some situations, we'd drop a pump into a nearby water source, like a pond or brook, then run hose to the fire and flank it. Other times, we'd try to create a barrier that the fire couldn't cross by digging out all the available fuel—trees, roots, brush, basically anything that will burn.

Fire is a fickle beast, and that's especially true with forest fires. The slightest shift in wind can send it howling in a completely different direction. That's what happened to us on that hot summer afternoon. We were positioned toward the top of a steep mountainside when all of a sudden fire started roaring up the slope.

There's an expression in firefighting: "attack from the black." Basically, it means the safest place to fight fires from is where the forest has already been burned through completely—the "black," as it's known. If you are completely surrounded by black, the fire has no fuel with which to move in your direction.

I looked back at our escape route that led back to "the black," but the bear was blocking our path. The shift in wind caused the fire to grow and spread more rapidly. It was quickly forming a semicircle around us. I kept working the fire's perimeter while keeping an eye on our narrowing escape route. That's when we got communication from the helicopter hovering overhead, with a clear visual of the riled-up bear on the hillside above us.

I don't know that I'd say it was a life-and-death moment, but I could feel my adrenaline surging as I worked to contain the fire around us. I did my best to remain calm and focus on the task at hand. "We need a bucket drop over here," the squad boss said over the radio. The bear was pacing anxiously near the edge of our narrow escape route, while the flames were coming fast and the ground underfoot was starting to erode. We kept digging out the fuel from the fire line trying to contain its spread and make another way out.

Just then, another helicopter appeared and dropped a bucket of water, about two thousand gallons' worth pulled from a nearby river, between us and the bear. That spooked the bear and sent him running back hard into the black, while extinguishing some of the nearby flames. With the bear out of the picture, there was just enough of an escape route to make our way to safety.

Five years later, while sitting in an office conference room in the Hurt Building in downtown Atlanta, I was reminded of that firefight on the mountaintop in Quebec. Not that the boardroom was life-threatening, but I still found myself planning my attack while also looking for my escape route, with not many good options.

To back up the story a bit, I'd come to Atlanta in the summer of 2012, shortly after fighting that Quebec fire in fact, to start a master's degree program in neurophilosophy at Georgia State University. My parents hadn't been thrilled with the decision. I remember when I first dropped the bomb on them that I was not going to med school. I was home from college for Thanksgiving break and we were driving to my sister Alaina's basketball game.

"So, I've decided I'm not going to go to medical school," I said, after gathering up the courage for about ten minutes. The silence was deafening.

"What are you going to do instead?" my mom asked.

"I want to be a philosophy professor, so I am going to apply to grad school for philosophy."

"You know, you won't make any money doing that," my mom said finally, after what felt like an eternity.

I'd been pre-med during my undergrad at Bates College in Maine, mostly because my parents wanted me to go to med school. They'd raised me well and I appreciated their guidance, but I'd never felt at home in the pre-med program.

"I'm sorry, Mom, but being a doctor just isn't my passion," I said.

"Well then, what is your passion?" she asked.

I did my best to explain that developing a deeper understanding of the mind, specifically the way in which the brain gives way to the mind, was the only thing truly exciting to me. Even as an eight-year-old boy, I was obsessed with the idea that you could control your mind through things like meditation and hypnosis. I even believed you could achieve almost supernatural powers by learning how to focus your mind and wrote a small book I called *The Book of the Mental Arts* complete with drawings of meditation focal points. Since then, I have dedicated much of my life to understanding how physical processes give rise to mental processes.

"Well, it's your decision," my dad chimed in, with a note of disappointment in his voice. "We want to make sure you are well off and you don't have to work forever until you can retire." I told them I had considered all my options and the process led me to the clear decision that a graduate program in philosophy, with an emphasis on neuroscience, was the next step in my academic journey.

That's how I ended up in Georgia at the age of twenty-two. I lived in a shotgun house in the Grant Park neighborhood of Atlanta with four other philosophy grad students. It was a time of partying and philosophizing. Most of the parties are a bit hazy, but I recall one particularly well. One of the guys in the house was turning twenty-five and we decided to have a "Fire and Ice" party. We made an ice luge for whiskey shots and built a huge bonfire in the backyard. The entire philosophy department showed up, along with their own guests. There were probably over sixty people crammed into the narrow house and around the fire outside. The air was thick with cigar and weed smoke. One of the guys was secretly dating one of his students (a surprisingly common occurrence) and had invited her to the party. I remember seeing her storm out the front door, while my housemate calmly lit up a cigarette and shrugged his shoulders. At one point in the night, everyone began chanting for me to rap, to which I eventually obliged. The drunken antics and intense debate raged on so long I don't remember sitting down in the armchair I woke up the next morning in.

My housemates and I used to argue 24/7 about everything and anything, from Kant to the nature of consciousness to the morality of eating animals. When there was nothing better to argue about, we'd debate whose turn it was to do the dishes.

I really enjoyed all the philosophical inquiry, but I was also getting more and more into the computational neuroscience side of things—to the increasing frustration of my philosophy professors. I remember telling my advisor that I wanted to write my thesis on what sort of algorithms and systems would have to be in place for a robot to be capable of emotions.

"Look, these algorithms are interesting and all," he said. "But your thesis really has to answer some kind of philosophical question."

I understood. But I also knew that my academic journey was pushing me deeper and deeper into the realm of artificial intelligence, or AI. I've mentioned my lifelong fascination with the human mind, going back to early childhood. I didn't want to spend my time theorizing about how cognitive systems worked anymore; I wanted to make them! The more I learned about the capacity for computers to simulate intelligence, and in the process solve even larger life problems, the more I knew I had found my true calling.

I realized there was so much good I could do with AI, including help in the fight against life-threatening diseases. This had been a mission of mine ever since I watched my grandmother lose her battle with Alzheimer's in 2000. I'll never forget visiting her in the hospital with my mom.

"Who are you?" Grandma said at one point, looking directly at her daughter of forty years. Even though my mom and I understood Alzheimer's debilitating effects on the brain, that was still a heartbreaking moment for my mom. When I saw the pain in her eyes, I vowed I would not let the same thing happen to her.

My worst fears came true when Mom was forced to endure her own gauntlet of illnesses, starting with breast cancer in 2012. Four rounds of chemotherapy were enough to send the cancer into remission, but it nearly took her life in the process. Seeing her unresponsive to Dad's and my attempts to talk to her in the hospital room after the last chemo treatment forced me to face the real possibility that she might perish. It was the hardest experience of my life.

Mom won the battle against breast cancer. However, we did not have long to celebrate before she started noticing she was having muscle tremors and difficulty with certain movements. At first, the doctors thought her sudden onset of tremors might be caused by something else. But my mom knew the truth, and after throwing myself into a crash course on Parkinson's disease I did as well.

My mom's health battles have been a test for our entire family, but her strength and fortitude are extraordinary. Her fights have brought our family closer together and given us all a deeper appreciation for life. Mom's health challenges also hardened my resolve to marshal whatever resources I could to fight these diseases.

I became more resolved to leveraging the power of AI in search of a cure or at least more effective treatments. In this sense, I knew I'd be coming back to the path of medicine that my parents wanted for me, but on my own terms.

That's how I ended up pursuing a second graduate degree at the Institute for Artificial Intelligence at the University of Georgia from 2014 to 2016. To the outside observer, it might have seemed like my goal was to become a career student, jumping from one discipline to the next, but I was very focused throughout this time on quantifying the human mind and learning how to re-create intelligence.

The scene at the AI institute was totally opposite from my experience in the philosophy program. Instead of constant debate and partying, everyone had their nose to the keyboard, writing code and studying algorithms, all day, every day. It was intense.

I lived in a seedy apartment complex my mom called the roach motel once while she was visiting. This was a more solitary time in my life, but I was okay with that because I was committed to the AI path. The only problem was I was struggling to pay my bills, since my research assistantship paid next to nothing. Out of desperation, I started checking out online job sites and discovered that I could make good money taking on freelance data science projects.

Over the next six months, I began building my reputation as a freelance data scientist and reached a point where I was hiring peers from the institute to help with larger projects. I eventually caught the attention of the CEO at a small financial software company that was looking to take a big step forward.

My phone buzzed one morning with a message from him, asking if we could chat about a potential opportunity. I gave him a call and he began describing the problem he was facing: his company had won a contract to build an anti-money-laundering system for a large financial services company, but he had no idea how to build it. He asked me how I would solve the problem. I described my solution, and when I was finished he offered me the job on the spot.

After the success of the anti-money-laundering system, I ended up hiring an entire team of data scientists and taking the lead as Chief Data Scientist. From there, it was hyper start-up mode, with me taking on increasing responsibilities, including opening two new offices in Atlanta. I found the spaces, set up the furniture, got the computers up and running, all while managing the team and developing the software. I was invested in this company. I felt like I had a hand in a lot of its early success. I was proud of the fact that I had pulled together this ragtag team of data scientists and had already built solutions to problems that were seen as intractable. I was only twenty-five and I was leading the charge against competitors many times our size and winning the "champion challenges" for the clients' contracts. Not only did I prove my leadership and vision to these clients, but I also proved them to myself.

At first, the CEO seemed to agree. But at a certain point I could sense a change. I felt like I was not getting credit where credit was due, and it seemed like he was trying to put me in my place. We had clashed horns several times over where our efforts were best placed, and I realized ultimately there was no persuading him. Still, I stuck with it, doing the work and bringing in more good people. My team secured a few big wins and I thought things were looking up.

That takes me back to the conference room in the Hurt Building. The CEO was not based in Atlanta, but he would fly into town a few times a month. It was on one of those visits that he asked for a private meeting. I reserved a room for us and waited for his arrival. I thought he was going to congratulate me for the team's recent successes and possibly even give me a raise.

Instead, I was met with scorn. You're not hiring the right people, he told me. You're not project-managing effectively. You're not saying the right things to clients. On and on he went for the better part of an hour.

There was some merit to his criticism: I *had* made some hiring mistakes. I prioritized projects I was interested in over others he felt were more important. I had stood my ground against clients who I felt were giving our team unreasonable deadlines. Still, I felt the wins my team and I had secured outweighed these mistakes. But the level of criticism was truly shocking. I took responsibility for these mistakes and highlighted my latest successes, but it all fell on deaf ears. It's not my style to storm out of any meeting, so I waited for him to run out of steam and then made my way out of the conference room, still trying to process what just happened. I knew from that point that my time with the company was limited. The fire was clearly closing in and I had fought it as long as I could. I had to make my way to the black.

After that letdown with the CEO, I started to check out more and more. I still showed up to work every day, but most of the time I'd shut the door to my office and work on whatever project interested me most. Lunch breaks got longer and longer. There were more coffee runs throughout the day.

One afternoon, I was coming back from one of those extended breaks when I noticed this long line of guys leading into my building. I went in for a closer look. They were all shuffling their feet, some looking around self-consciously, while others were puffing up their chests. There was a guy with a clipboard standing near the front of the line who seemed to be in charge.

"Hey, what's going on here?" I asked him.

"Casting call for a reality show," he answered.

"Oh yeah, what's it about?" I asked.

"It's a dating show called *Married at First Sight: Second Chances*," he said. "A man and woman whose spouses left them are going to be dating a group of eligible singles to see if they can find the one."

"What could go wrong?" I joked.

"Exactly," he said with a devilish grin. "You interested?"

"Nah," I told him. "I have a girlfriend."

"Well, if it doesn't work out, let us know," he said.

"Will do," I said, and made my way back into the building, already depressed at the thought of returning to the boredom and frustration that awaited me there. As I turned through the revolving glass door, I caught a reflection of the line of guys waiting for their chance at love. A small sliver of me wanted to keep turning through the door and walk to the back of that line. I started to fantasize about the adventure of a new reality but, for the time being, resolved myself to focusing on the current one.

chapter three

ALWAYS MR. WRONG

Lauren

I stared at the DM in my inbox, half laughing at it. Though life after thirty was looking up for me in many ways, dating was not one of them. The message was from a casting agent. "Hey, there's a new dating show filming in Atlanta and I think you would be a great fit," she wrote, or something to that effect.

"Really?" I said to myself. "I'd say my dating life sucks."

Allow me to explain.

When it comes to dating, I was a late bloomer. I didn't have my first boyfriend until my sophomore year in college. I've always been very goal oriented. I focused on extracurricular activities, dance recitals, or theater practice. Romance seemed like such a gamble.

Like most kids affected by their parents' divorce, I was reluctant to chase love. I had just graduated from college when they officially split, after seventeen years of marriage. My mom and dad had been separated for several years, but they would see each other from time to time and still seemed to be friends. Deep down I was holding on to the hope that one day they could get back together, but when I returned home from college my mom came into my room to give me the news that this was not going to happen. Perhaps my graduating was a time marker for them both. They finally had to admit that if a reconciliation hadn't happened yet, it probably never would.

"I know that this is upsetting," my mother said, "but I went through with the divorce from your father."

Even though they had been separated for a while, and I was an adult at that point, her words hit me like a punch in the chest. Except this hit would take me more than a decade to resolve.

Some of my early struggles in dating were remnants of what I believed to be unresolved feelings surrounding my parents' split.

Take my first relationship in college, for example. My boyfriend was this big, charismatic guy, member of the football team, and larger than life. Laughing was our second language. We'd crack jokes and binge-watch *Martin*.

He had a child from an earlier relationship, a little girl who was around two at the time. While the situation was challenging, we made it work for a year, more or less. At least, I thought we were making it work. One morning, we had met up and I could tell something was up right away. There was no sparkle in his eye, none of the easy laughter.

"What is it?" I said.

"You're an amazing woman, Lauren," he started.

Uh-oh, I thought.

"It's just that it's really important to be in my daughter's life," he continued. "And in order to do that, I'd like to heal my relationship with her mother. You have so much strength and talent. I know you're going to be fine. The best thing for me to do is to let you go."

I felt that punch to my chest again, and it sent me into a downward spiral for weeks. I couldn't stop wondering what was wrong with *me*. What had I done to mess things up? Because I had such a fragile view of relationships, I internalized everything and came away more insecure than when I entered the relationship. The experience also left me with further trust issues. Could he have been seeing the child's mother the entire time we were dating?

This set a pattern that I would repeat throughout my twenties. It always came back to trust. Anytime I felt myself getting happy in a relationship, I would pull back emotionally because I knew it was only a matter of time before the letdown. Not gonna lie, every time I experienced a failed romance, thoughts of my parents' divorce tapped me on the shoulder. I had to do whatever it took to protect myself from that disappointment.

I became a consecutive long-distance dater. It was another defense mechanism I had developed. It was a way to avoid being too intimate and too vulnerable. I've often wondered if there is any correlation between this and the fact that my dad traveled often for work when I was growing up. In turn, I had to learn to love people from a distance. I'd watch my girlfriends get involved with men and develop instant connections. Mind you, it didn't always last. But part of me wished that I could learn to be less protective.

Unfortunately, the men I met in Atlanta were rarely what I was looking for. When the girls and I would step out, there were always guys lurking. We'd hang out around town, sip our sidecars, and comment on the procession of bachelors. Some were okay, but inevitably they'd turn out to be shallow or boring. Tiff and I always had our eye-lock distress signal that meant "Mayday! Send help!" To me, the Atlanta dating scene was difficult to navigate and lackluster. Doing the long-distance thing was a way to keep the Atlanta gents at bay.

My last relationship before *Love Is Blind* perfectly represented all this. He and I had gone to college together and then reconnected a few years later online. He was living in Los Angeles at the time, working in entertainment. The relationship started with a few flirty DMs. Within a week we were texting every day.

We had a lot of similarities—creative, driven, and motivated. As I had grown up witnessing my father being a go-getter, that became a quality I admired and appreciated in men. My ex fit the mold for the type of men I had always found myself drawn to.

He had a lot of positive qualities and a drive for success. He had a sweet, calm, caring personality, which was different from the brash, arrogant types I had fallen for in the past. We talked about our businesses and life goals but also fun, easygoing stuff, like our latest binge on Netflix or places we wanted to travel.

This went on for over a year. We'd fly out to see each other every few weeks and communicate by phone, text, or DMs the rest of the time. It felt like a serious relationship. And then, as had happened every time before, the bottom sort of fell out.

We used to call or text every day, even if it was just a heart emoji. One week, a couple days went by without any communication. So I texted him but no response. The next day, I called. He answered, but the conversation was stale and distant. This happened to be right around the time of his ex's birthday. With a sinking feeling in my stomach, I went onto her Instagram page, and sure enough, there was my guy sitting next to her at her party.

The next day, the relationship ended. Would you believe he did it over text? I thought, *You couldn't even call me? Dang!* As if the medium of the breakup wasn't bad enough, the timing couldn't have been worse—it was the fall of 2017, right around the time my business was failing and I was having to borrow money from my parents to make the rent.

As I explained earlier, I was able to pull myself up by my bootstraps with my work life. But as 2018 rolled around, the only love I wanted to think about was self-love. I went out on a few dates here and there, in keeping with the whole *living my life to the fullest* thing. But any thoughts of settling down were on permanent hold.

I wondered which part of my tired love life the *LIB* casting agent thought made me a perfect fit for her new dating show. But I wasn't about to write her back and find out. Me and dating were done for a while. It was time to pack my bags again and go see more of the world.

chapter four

PEER PRESSURES

Cameron

The situation with the CEO had shaken me from my complacency and forced me to examine all aspects of my life—including my love life. I realized there were many parallels between my professional and romantic lives. In both worlds, it was becoming clear to me that the end was approaching.

Before the age of twenty-eight, I had three degrees under my belt, I was making a name for myself in the increasingly in-demand field of AI, and I'd opened two offices for a growing tech company. But, as I've described, the appearance did not match my reality: I was miserable going into work every day, I felt like my talents were not being appreciated, and I knew I needed to find the next step in my career, but I was not making moves to change my situation.

As I took stock of my dating life, I noticed something: in both my career and my personal relationship, I knew I was unhappy in the wrong situation, but I resisted ending the relationship because I didn't want to be alone and lose what I had worked so hard to maintain. I realized that if I was ever going to find enduring happiness and fulfillment, I needed to take responsibility for my well-being and have enough faith in myself to leap into the unknown and thrive.

After five years and many breakups, I finally committed to ending the relationship with the woman I had been seeing. In the months after the breakup, I spent most of my time alone, reflecting on how I needed to practice more compassion toward myself and how important it was to set my expectations up front for future relationships, personal or professional. I realized that it was necessary to spend that time alone to learn how to be content by myself, though at the same time I longed for intimacy.

The truth is, I've always been a lover. Even as a young kid, when most of the boys were running away from girls and their cooties, I was writing them love notes. I couldn't wait to have a girlfriend. My hometown of Lee, Maine, has a population of around eight hundred, so it isn't exactly a teenage dating paradise. But it is unique in that the town is home to Lee Academy, a semi-private boarding and day high school with an international dorm that attracts students from all over the world.

That's how it came to pass that in the ninth grade I finally got my first girlfriend—a visiting student from South Korea. Not only was she from a different country; she was a senior at the school, which made her four years older. I was tall for my age, which helped give the impression we were closer in age. Regardless, it was the mixed-race part of the relationship that everyone focused on, often with the negative judgment they were ready to share.

"Oh, he's into Asian girls," one of the guys in the locker room said while imitating a Korean accent. Most of the comments I received were from other guys on the soccer team, as my girlfriend managed the team's equipment and scorecard. One day, as I was walking to join the others on the field before soccer practice, one of the guys yelled out, "Hey, dude, how's the yellow fever?" Many in the huddled group laughed. Another time, a junior from the team passed me in the hall and whispered, "You know she's only dating you for a green card."

"That's not true!" I replied through my clenched jaws, but the upperclassman just chuckled to himself and walked away. I let my balled-up fist relax as he disappeared from view.

I was angry and frustrated by how people were mocking our relationship. I was ready to fight anyone who had something negative to say about us, and would let them know that type of bigoted talk was wrong. I also didn't understand why people had such a hard time processing why I wanted to date her. From my perspective, I'd spent my entire life with the same twenty or so girls from town who were in my class. The chance to go out with someone new was exciting. Of course, I was aware of the fact that she was Korean, but that wasn't my motivation for dating her. I was also aware that it was unusual for a senior girl to date a freshman boy. I didn't care about her age and she always felt the need to reassure me (or perhaps herself) that I was more mature than the guys in her class.

Everyone else was clearly not convinced.

Obviously, it didn't work out—I was fourteen years old! And she moved back to Korea. But what I took away from the experience was that people are always ready to weigh in on your relationship, whether you ask for their opinion or not. While I ignored the opinions that were clearly based in prejudice, I still allowed others to weigh in on my dating life. In times when my relationship was in turmoil, I found myself seeking friends' and family's advice rather than listening to my own intuition. When I asked those closest to me what I should do about my long-distance relationship with my first girlfriend, the unanimous response was that I should let her go. That wasn't what I wanted to hear, so naturally I resisted as long as I could until we both knew it wasn't going to work. I wanted my support system to tell me everything was going to be all right, but I refused to listen when I didn't get the feedback I wanted.

That pattern of allowing others to weigh in would be repeated over the decade of dating that followed. In that time, I went out with women from many different backgrounds and of different ethnicities. One of my girlfriends in college at Bates was a blond volleyball player from California. Another was a pre-med student and a dancer from Vietnam. I also dated a girl from Lebanon whose art I admired. For me, it was exciting to form connections with people who had different backgrounds than me and who could expand my world.

From an early age, I always looked at the issue of inequality in an empirical way. There is nothing inherently different in one person or one race or ethnicity. People are fundamentally all the same and they should be treated the same way. As I got older, I came to realize that the issue is a little more complicated than that—or a lot more complicated.

My college dating life ended on a strange note. With a month left in my senior year, I met a girl in the philosophy club. We started chatting and hit it off immediately. I'm a romantic at heart, so I've always been the type to fall hard and fast. With so little time left at school, we were on an accelerated track, so we ended up being intimate within the first week; I don't tend to move that quickly, but with the clock ticking on my college days, we both felt like there was no time to waste.

That's when she told me she had a boyfriend.

"Wow . . . okay," I said. "You definitely need to end it with him if we're going to keep seeing each other. I really like you and I want to keep seeing you after I graduate, but you have to break up with him if you want that too."

"I will; I promise," she said.

I got a call from her the next day: "Hey, guess what? I broke it off with him. He didn't want to accept it and he got really angry. I'm so done with him."

"I'm so happy to hear that. Don't worry about him. I'll make sure nothing happens to you."

"I'm kind of scared right now. Can I come over?"

"Yeah, of course."

Fast-forward a few weeks; we were in her dorm room and things were heating up. All of a sudden, there was a pounding at the door. Her ex-boyfriend had come by to collect his things. The door was locked, so he started slamming his body against it, as he'd heard my voice inside the room.

She started sobbing and telling him to go away, while I rushed to get dressed. "You're a slut! You're a bitch!" he screamed through the door. My heart was racing out of my chest as I swung open the door, ready for a fight.

"Who the fuck are you?" he snarled, shoving me back into the room. I grabbed him by the neck and we started to brawl. She called campus security as we fought, and within a minute they were on the scene to separate us. It was an ugly situation and it only got worse later when he continued to berate her over text. The whole experience raised a red flag in the back of my mind. I asked myself, "Was I in the wrong for seeing her so close after she said she ended things with her boyfriend?" "Should I have waited?" But I ignored these thoughts and pressed on, trying to convince myself of the romance of our relationship rather than focusing on how problematic it was.

After graduation, we continued to date long-distance. I flew out to see her on the West Coast once and she came out to Maine. But the distance was taking a toll. After three months of not seeing each other, she called to say that she thought we should break up. I was devastated by the news and tried to figure out what I had done wrong and how I could fix our relationship. I soon realized, however, that there wasn't anything to fix.

Fortunately, a fresh start awaited me in Atlanta.

I'd been in Atlanta a couple months, still sulking over my latest breakup. At a certain point, I decided it was time to stop feeling sorry for myself. I was in a new city filled with amazing women. It was time to get back out there.

I woke up one morning and said to myself, "You are going to talk to five new women today and every day until you find someone you really connect with." I had come to the conclusion that I needed to let go of my inhibitions and take a chance with the women I found myself attracted to. I wasn't going to wait and pray for the universe to create those situations for me; I was going to create them myself! I got out of bed with a renewed sense of conviction and went about my day.

The first woman I talked to had caught my attention on the way to my philosophy of mind class on the downtown campus of Georgia State University. I tried to pretend we were in class together and asked her about an assignment. She just looked at me in confusion, told me she wasn't in that class, and walked away. Swing and a miss!

The second woman I met in the health center at school while waiting to get a flu shot. We started up a conversation about photography, but I didn't feel much chemistry between us. I left without asking for her phone number. It was another miss, but I felt my anxiety starting to reduce to a simmer.

I was walking back home when I noticed a woman who really caught my eye. She was a Black woman with nice curves and a confident stride. We were crossing the street together, so I quickly racked my brain for something to say. I still needed to talk to three more women, right?

"Hey, I like your bag," I said.

"Oh, thank you," she replied. "My sister is a designer and she made it."

We continued chatting as we walked toward the library together.

"Where's your class?" she asked as we reached the library courtyard.

"It's actually in the opposite direction," I said, with a laugh. "But I wanted to get to know you." As we were about to part ways, she held out her phone for me to enter my number into, right as I was about to do the same thing.

"Some of my friends and I are getting drinks later tonight at

Anatolia's. You're welcome to come," she said after I finished typing in my number. *Mission accomplished*, I thought.

I turned up at the bar a few hours later. She was there with some friends. One by one the group filtered away until it was just the two of us. I thought that was an encouraging sign. At the point when I thought this was becoming a date, she said, "You would be great for my sister."

"Your sister?" I replied. "What about you?"

"You're sweet, Cameron," she said. "But I have a boyfriend."

We talked for a few hours longer before heading our separate ways. I felt a strong, instant connection with her and I knew she felt it too. She spent a significant part of the night talking about all the ways her boyfriend wasn't making her happy. So why was she still with him? Why did I keep finding myself in these situations where I was attracted to someone on the outs with her partner? I went home feeling both accomplished for my initiative and unsure of what to make of this new connection.

I tried to forget about her, thinking back on how badly things had gone last time I got in the middle of someone's relationship. About a week later, she texted: "My friend makes the best mixed drinks. Want to come by?" Several changes of plans later, she arrived at my place.

"So I have to tell you something," she began.

"What's that?"

"I broke up with my boyfriend yesterday. He said something racist to me and it was the final straw."

"Oh? I'm so sorry to hear that."

"No you're not! Look at you—look at how hard you're smiling!"

"I'm sorry to hear he said something racist to you. Clearly he doesn't deserve you."

"It's fine. We don't have to talk about him anymore."

"Great. Let's talk about us then."

The rest was . . . well, the rest was five years of what I think is best described as a learning experience.

I have thought at great length about how to discuss this relationship. On the one hand, I've decided it does not make sense to rehash every detail of the highs and lows we went through. What happened is in the past now, and I do not want to spend much time recounting what we both had to heal from. On the other hand, this was the five years of my life immediately preceding *Love Is Blind*, and I do want to tell you a few things the relationship taught me.

First, it's hard to love and respect someone else when you do not love and respect yourself. This was a problem we both had to face. During this time, I did not have enough respect for my needs to fully communicate them to her. I was afraid that bringing up difficult issues would lead to a fight, and I didn't want to deal with the consequences of that. However, in not having the courage to bring up these issues, the problems only festered and led to bigger problems down the road. I learned it's better to bring up issues to your partner right away, even if it leads to some temporary tension between you. The longer you wait, the greater potential for the problem to mature into something much harder to solve, like resentment toward your partner.

Second, I learned not to romanticize relationships with frequent cycles of breakups and make-ups. In books and movies, I had observed that often the star-crossed lovers of the story would have some dramatic argument, which would result in a period of separation, until one of the lovers made a grand romantic gesture and all was forgiven. When our relationship went through these same cycles, I simply told myself that this was normal. Over time, I became hooked on the rush of rekindling the relationship after a period of separation, rather than acknowledging the fundamental issues we needed to resolve. I think in a healthy relationship, both partners need to feel secure enough in the relationship that they feel comfortable arguing with their partner without worrying that it will end the relationship.

Third, I learned it's not fundamentally wrong to argue in relationships—rather it's the way you and your partner argue that matters. You often hear that even healthy couples argue and that is true. But it's the way that a couple argues that differentiates a healthy relationship from an unhealthy relationship. When couples in a healthy relationship argue, they acknowledge their partner's point of view and try to empathize with them. Even when things get heated they focus on how they can both work to resolve the problem together, rather than on what their partner did wrong. They address issues as they come up; they do not bottle their feelings up until they explode. We had not yet learned how to argue in a healthy way, and we hurt each other as a result. The good news is that it's possible to learn how to argue in a healthy way. I think this starts with a shared willingness by both parties to address problems when they first occur and a shared focus on resolving the problem together and listening to and acknowledging your partner's perspective. When you and your partner both feel heard and respected, rather than ignored and criticized, you will both be more willing to work to a solution.

Finally, you need to trust your gut when it comes to when to end a relationship and not let outside factors influence your judgment. I had recognized for a long time that my ex and I were not right for each other, but I came up with reasons to stay in the relationship. One of the biggest reasons was that I had become close with her family. However, no matter how close I became to her family, it would not resolve the underlying issues in our relationship. When I finally acknowledged what my gut was telling me, I made the healthiest decision for us both and I ended the relationship. It allowed me to make space in my life for what was about to happen with *Love Is Blind*.

A few months after breaking things off with my ex, I took my team out for a work lunch. We were at a popular Vietnamese spot in downtown Atlanta called Dua. There were six of us seated at a table in their basement that reminded me of *Blade Runner* with its funky lights and decorations. I was about to tuck into my lemongrass beef and rice when my phone buzzed with a text from an unknown number.

The message was pretty suspect: it looked like some kind of ad, complete with a stock image of a man and woman holding hands while looking into each other's eyes. My first thought was that it must be spam. As I looked more closely at the image in the text, I realized it was some kind of casting call. "Are you looking for true love?" it read. "Do you want to find the perfect someone without the superficial elements of dating?"

I thought back to my encounter with the *Married at First Sight* casting agent outside my office building. Had I given him my number? I couldn't recall. But why else would I be getting this weird text out of the blue? I showed the message to a couple members of my team at the table.

"How crazy is this?"

"Oh, you should definitely do it!" one of them shouted.

"Yeah, right," I said. "Like I'm going to find the love of my life on a reality show."

I put my phone away and got back to my beef and rice.

Ridiculous, I thought to myself. But as much as I tried to dismiss the idea, I couldn't help thinking that maybe it was time to try something new in my dating life. I wasn't making connections on the dates I went on through the apps and was up for an adventure. I could not think about anything else for the rest of the day.

chapter five

PLAYING HARD TO GET

Lauren

I was actually researching flights to Paris when the little arrow appeared on my Instagram app. Being no stranger to the ways of social media, I probably had six or seven thousand followers at that time, so random DMs were pretty common. Some were promising business leads, while others were annoying interruptions—a pointless spam ad maybe, or a creepy compliment from a random guy. I ignored it for a few hours. Later that night, I was lying in bed, scrolling through my messages. That's when I realized that the latest DM was another follow-up from *Love Is Blind*.

I was still hesitant to start a conversation about being on a dating show at first. But the casting agent who had sent the original DM was very persistent; perhaps she combed through my social media and felt I'd be a great addition to the group of interesting personalities they were compiling. There were plenty of posts on my feed of me and the ladies enjoying nights out, posed in our group selfies.

Anyway, the casting agent's latest message went something like: "Take a look at it. Give me your email address so that I can send you more information."

I thought back to all the praying I'd done over the last six months or so. Something in my heart was telling me that maybe this was some kind of divine intervention at play. *Maybe.*

What's the worst that could happen? I thought. *This is crazy, but let's just see what happens.*

The application hit my inbox pretty much instantly. I took my time filling it out. Dating reality shows are a dime a dozen in Atlanta—a few of the big production companies are based there, so the opportunity still didn't feel very special. But then the casting agent and I spoke, and she explained the whole concept of the show, including the fact that we'd be going on dates without actually *seeing* the other person.

That sparked my interest. You see, at a certain point in my mid-twenties I started to lean into my sapiosexuality—you know, the act of being turned on by intelligence and deep, meaningful conversation. (What did you think it meant?? Lol!) After so many years of focusing on physical attributes—the six-pack abs, tall and strapping physique—I decided to base my attraction on what the mind of a man looked like. It doesn't matter how gorgeous he is; if he's a coldhearted asshole with the emotional intelligence of a jellyfish, it's not going to get far. But if he asks me thoughtful questions or makes interesting observations, that's when something clicks for me.

So the concept of *Love Is Blind* appealed to that side of my dating personality. I liked the idea that the relationships wouldn't be based on anything physical, at least not in the beginning. Plus, this was during my whole *Eat, Pray, Love* journey, which was centered around being connected to myself and the world. It all kind of felt right.

I agreed to more interviews with the casting agents. I was intrigued, but I definitely wasn't desperate to make the cut, so I had no trouble being my regular, goofy self. I made a few jokes that I remember had the casting lady in tears. I was thinking to myself, *Wait, I'm not that funny. This lady's laughing way too hard.*

The agents contacted me again to say the producers loved me and they wanted to move forward with the process, which involved filling out these long-ass psych evaluations, with a bunch of questions that seemed to be designed to make sure you're not the type to stab someone in the eye with a stiletto if they look at you the wrong way. I swear the first questionnaire was thirteen pages long. And that was just the beginning!

At some point in the process I let my mom and dad in on what was happening. Their initial reaction was what you'd expect from any rational parents.

"What are you doing that for?" my dad asked.

My mom was also skeptical at first, but she was a little quicker to come around. "Your dad is right; it is crazy," she said during one of our weekly calls. "But who knows, you just might fall in love and find a husband." This was one of my mom's favorite themes. I knew exactly what was coming next. "Because you know, you're not getting any younger," she added in the next breath.

Boom! There it was.

"Yeah, I thought you might say that, Mom," I said, biting my tongue.

"Well, I'm sorry, but you're thirty years old," she continued.

"Eggs don't last forever, you know. What are you going to do, live the rest of your life alone?"

"Oh my God, Mom!" I cried. "It's the twenty-first century! Not all women are married with children by the age of twenty-five. In fact, not all women even want to get married or have children."

Like I said, this was one of our routine discussions, so it was mostly a lot of teasing. Though I knew my mom was serious about wanting me to find love and start a family of my own. Even though I'd resigned myself to the single life, a small part of me wanted that too.

Throughout that summer of 2018, I'd hear every now and then from the producers. But work was picking up and I was staying busy. So I didn't give much thought to *Love Is Blind*. Plus, I knew from my work as a model that you could be out of the running anytime. It could be the day before a shoot when someone from Creative decides they want a girl with a different look. And that's it; you're out. It happens all the time.

Once or twice I checked in with the producers. "I'm filling out all these forms and paperwork," I'd say. "Did I make it?"

"Well, you know, we can't quite confirm anything yet," they'd respond. "But they really like you!"

Mm-hmm, I'd think to myself.

That was just fine with me. I was super excited for my upcoming trip to Paris. Cuba and Italy had been solo missions, but this time I'd have a traveling companion, none other than my friend Tiffany. It was only a five-day trip in September, but we'd been planning it for months. We had found this amazing Airbnb in the 1st arrondissement of Paris, walking distance from the Louvre. It had one of those balconies that looked out over the city. There was even a bakery right below us, so we'd wake up each morning to the aroma of fresh-baked baguettes.

Our trip coincided with Fashion Week. I have an older cousin who lives in Paris and she came to see us one day. She was floored. "How did you get this place in this neighborhood during Fashion Week?" she asked in disbelief. "That just doesn't happen."

Tiff and I had a ball living our best single girl lives in the most beautiful city in the world. Our second night there we even ended up scoring tickets to the L'Oréal Fashion Week party. The place was crawling with supermodels and they were giving out free bottles of champagne. At one point the DJ put on "I Will Survive" and this gorgeous supermodel grabbed me and shouted, "Dance with me!" I danced all night, drinking champagne and lapping up the energy and excitement. It was one of the greatest nights of my life.

A few nights later, a Friday, Tiffany and I were at the Eiffel Tower. It was one of those perfect autumn evenings. Paris was sparkling, and I fully understood why they call it the City of Lights. We were about to leave the tower for dinner when my phone rang. It was an LA number.

It had been more than a week since my last contact with the producers and several months since I was first contacted about the show. I'd been fighting the thought of allowing myself to get excited about the possible opportunity from the beginning, but in my heart of hearts I wanted to make the cut. I just didn't want to get my hopes up, since I knew that even sure things could be snatched away at the last minute. As I stared down at the 310 area code, my body went cold and my heart started pounding in my chest.

"Hello, who's this?" I said, trying to sound as nonchalant as possible.

"Hi, Lauren, this is the producer from *Love Is Blind*," the caller responded. "Guess what? You made the show!"

I was speechless.

"Filming starts Monday," she continued. "Can you be ready?"

"Wait, what? I'm in Paris right now!" I shouted, my mind already swimming with panicked thoughts about my lackluster wardrobe and how I was possibly going to squeeze in a mani-pedi *and* a transatlantic flight in the next seventy-two hours.

"Listen, we'd love to have you in the mix," the producer said. "See what you can do."

Mon Dieu.

chapter six

EYE OF THE TIGER

Cameron

My spring of 2018 was marked by a lot of frustration, first with the CEO I worked for, then with my longtime girlfriend. Heading into summer, I was ready for a fresh start. It had been a couple weeks since the random text message in the restaurant. As intrigued as I had been by it, I hadn't responded.

After stepping out of the shower one morning, I saw a missed call on my phone. I listened to the voice message.

"I'm casting for a new dating show with a really cool premise. If you're interested, give me a call back."

My curiosity got the best of me.

"Hey, this is Cameron Hamilton," I said.

"Cameron, I'm so happy you called," he said casually, as if we'd known each other forever.

"Yeah, for sure! I was intrigued by the message you left."

"Right on, man!"

". . . So tell me more about this show," I said cautiously.

"It's a dating show for Netflix," he started. "They haven't committed to a title yet, but they're thinking of calling it *Love Is Blind*."

"Wait, Netflix?" I interrupted. I had been assuming it was some obscure network or maybe an overseas production company I had never heard of.

"Oh yeah, it's big-time," the casting agent continued. "Think *The Bachelor*, only there will be an even number of men and women, probably fifteen or twenty. Oh, and you won't be able to see each other until you're engaged."

"Engaged? Wow . . . that's . . . that's . . . something," I said. It was a lot to process all at once. At the time, I was thinking, *Who would be foolish enough to propose to someone they've never seen after two weeks of talking to them?*

"And I can assure you everyone is very well rounded," he added, breaking the silence. At this point, I wasn't thinking about the quality of the women who might be cast. Even though I was the one to call him back, I couldn't believe I was having a conversation about being on a dating show and that at least a small part of me was entertaining it. It's true I was hungry for adventure: my work life was disappointing and my dating life wasn't much better. But this idea of truly blind dating went against all laws of attraction as I understood them.

He went on to describe the premise of the show: There would be two weeks of blind dating, with a wall separating the men from the women. The potential partners would be able to talk to each other on one-on-one dates through the wall but would not be able to see each other. Couples who made a connection would have the chance to propose through the wall. If their partner accepted, they would go on a "proposal-moon," spend a few weeks living together, then have an actual wedding.

"You still there?" he said, after an extended period of silence on my end.

"Sorry, yeah, sounds fascinating," I said, by which I meant it sounded totally insane. "Isn't that all very fast, though?"

"It is," he agreed. "But that's the experiment. And hey, listen, no pressure. But think about it. If you're interested, I'll send you the initial application form. You can drop out at any point during the process."

"Okay," I said. "I guess there's no harm in that."

I hung up the phone and stood there in a wet towel in the middle of my bedroom for about five minutes, thinking to myself, *What are you getting yourself into?*

I obviously filled out the form. Within a few days, the casting agent called back to set up a Skype interview. "So the women in our casting office are excited at the possibility of having you on the show, but we want to do a video interview so we can get a better sense of your personality." He asked about my past dating life, my current career situation, and even my wildest stories from college.

Toward the end of the call, he asked me to read off some sound bites for the camera. He told me it was a good way for Casting to see how I looked and sounded on camera. The one I remember best was when he had me say, "I'm just a nerdy white rapper from Maine who wants to save the world through artificial intelligence."

I burst out laughing when he gave me the line.

"You really want me to say that?"

"Yeah, I know it's kind of corny, but it's fun, right?"

I hesitated, then gave in. "Oh, what the hell. Why not?"

I delivered the line and the agent ate it up. And that was it.

A few weeks went by. I did my best to put the show out of my mind. My job at least provided a distraction, but the further I proceeded through the casting process, the more invested I became. My office overlooked downtown Atlanta, and I'd often catch myself looking out the window, daydreaming about the experiment. I tried to imagine what the pods Production kept talking about would look like, what it would be like to date through a wall, and where I would fit into the world of reality television. I even started considering the possibility that I could actually connect with someone through this whole love experiment.

My initial skepticism about *Love Is Blind* was clearly fading. Nevertheless, I continued to date during this time, though I started to feel guilty about it once I realized I actually had a chance of getting cast. I was transparent about this possibility on the dates but played down the likelihood of it, mostly because I was trying to convince myself not to get too invested in the show. I quickly realized that I could not get invested in the dates either, and that it wasn't fair to anyone.

The casting agent eventually reached back out to say I made it to the next round. That meant filling out multiple personality tests with hundreds of questions each, along the lines of *Why do you think your past relationships have failed?* and *What have your friends and family said about your past relationships?* and *How do you know that you are in love with someone?*

I even had to do an in-person psych evaluation. The assessment took place way out in the suburbs in this nondescript psychiatry institute. I remember walking through these dark, empty corridors. It all felt very ominous. Eventually, I found my way to a conference room and took a seat. Other guys started to filter in, maybe a dozen in all.

I looked around the room to see who else was going on this crazy journey with me. I noticed a guy on the other side of the room. He was wearing a sports jersey and shorts. I could tell he was amused by my suit. As we exited the conference room, he turned and said, "Hey, man, nice suit," while chuckling to himself. I laughed too. That guy would turn out to be none other than Matt Barnett.

I completed the written portion of the evaluation and was called into the next room for a face-to-face with a trained psychologist. She started asking me questions about my early childhood and how I was raised, then proceeded to assess my full history of interpersonal relationships up until the present day. I was seriously drained by the end of it.

Another couple of weeks passed without hearing much from Casting. At this point, I was becoming borderline obsessed. Something inside was telling me this was the right path; this was what I was meant to be doing right now. I finally let my parents in on the secret. While I had told them about the initial casting phone call, I had originally assured them I wasn't going to pursue it. A couple months had passed since that conversation, and I had not told them how far I had progressed through the casting process. As expected, my mom was none too pleased.

I believe her precise words were, "Don't do it, Cameron. Please, I don't want you to do it."

"Come on, Mom, why not?" I asked playfully.

"It's flattering that they think so highly of you," she answered. "But there's a very good chance that you'll end up hurt and humiliated."

My dad remained neutral. "I don't think it's a great idea," he said. "But it's your decision."

While some of my family and friends supported my journey through the casting process, such as my godbrothers Sam and Thomas and my friend Shervin, the majority of those I told about this dating experiment discouraged me from participating. There is a pervasive negative impression of reality television in our culture. Some of that negativity toward reality television is warranted—sometimes people act ridiculous or unpredictably when they're put in front of a camera in some strange situation. Often, Casting seems to seek out people they believe will bring the drama with them. Other times, the magic of editing may obscure the truth. Either way, my loved ones seemed to think there was a decent chance I could come away from this looking like a fool.

One of the only friends in my corner was my friend Ben, whom I'd met during my philosophy grad program. He had been witness to the trials and tribulations of my last relationship and had helped me process how to handle the low points. He never told me I needed to leave her, but he was honest about when he thought the relationship sounded unhealthy. When I told him about the experiment, he couldn't contain his excitement.

"You're perfect for this," he said.

"It's strange, though. I don't fit the mold of your standard guy who goes on these types of shows."

"Exactly, dude. That's why you have to do it. Think about it—

you're a sensitive guy and you're articulate about your feelings. And I know you're actually going to take this seriously. You have to do it, dude. And besides, what's the worst that could happen?"

I took Ben's words to heart. But I also started to allow myself to ask the question, *What's the best that could happen?* The further along I got into the casting process, the more I started to feel as if everything that was unfolding with the show was meant to be. What started as skepticism was quickly turning into a feeling that fate was running its course.

While I still had not been officially picked for the cast, I was presented with an intense contract. By this time, the casting agent had handed me over to one of the field producers.

"This contract is scary," I said to him during one of my many check-in calls.

"Oh yeah, don't worry about that," he said. "It's boilerplate stuff. Even if you're just going on *Family Feud*, they make you sign a contract like that. The most important thing is you just be yourself and don't try to be someone you think we want you to be. People who try to act wild and crazy because they think that's what producers want to see get portrayed as wild and crazy."

I had discussions with the producer and some of the other staff in Production, and they did their best to alleviate my concerns by emphasizing that even clever editing cannot make something out of nothing. While I was not entirely convinced, I was already way deep into my leap of faith, so I decided to press on with the casting process. Besides, I knew the whole thing could still fall apart at any time.

I tried to stay defensively pessimistic about my chances of getting cast. In my heart, I wanted it more each day. If I'd been phoning it in at work before, now I was completely checked out. I've always taken pride in working hard and getting the job done, but I just could not bring myself to care anymore.

August turned into September. It had been three months since the first text message from the casting agent came through while I was out to lunch at the Vietnamese restaurant. I knew that October 1 was the official start date for production, so I was starting to get anxious, despite the reassurances from the producer that everyone at Netflix and Kinetic really liked me.

One day toward the middle of the month, I gave Ben a call to see if he wanted to meet for a beer after work. The anticipation was getting to me. I thought it would be good to blow off a little steam. We made a plan to meet at Moe's & Joe's Tavern a few miles from my office.

It was around six o'clock and I was in my car driving to the bar. I came to a red light and looked down at my phone. There was a message from the producer.

"You're officially in! CONGRATULATIONS!!!" it said, with a bunch of champagne bottle emojis.

Even in my most excited state, I'm a pretty calm guy. But when I saw that message, I completely lost it. I started banging the steering wheel with the palm of my hand and cheering louder than I had cheered for anything before. Whoever might have been watching in that moment probably thought I'd come completely unhinged.

In a sense, the opposite was true. I hadn't become unhinged from reality—far from it, I had just been cast on a reality show!

But in that moment, I knew that my life had just changed forever. I could not wait to see where this dating experiment would take me.

Training Days

Though I was skeptical at first about *Love Is Blind*, as soon as I came around to the idea, I was all in. That resulted in several months of intensive mental and physical preparation (even though I didn't get the final green light until a couple weeks before the start of shooting, I wanted to be well ready, just in case). I was not oblivious to the fact that thousands, maybe even millions of people would be watching the show and forming their own judgments about me. I definitely wanted to look and feel my best for the cameras. I also wanted to look my best for myself, and on the slim chance that I connected with someone, my future partner. The preparation was not just about appearances, however. I truly believed that the more I put into the experience, the more I stood to gain. I think that's a good rule to follow for all pursuits in life, including the pursuit of a meaningful relationship.

So, what did my training regime look like?

While I had seen reality TV shows before, I did not know much about dating shows. I wanted to get a sense of what I was in for, so I started watching shows like *Bachelor in Paradise* and *Married at First Sight*. I quickly realized that I have a very different personality than those I saw represented on these shows. Often the men and women tend to be over-the-top and in constant competition with one another for the spotlight. You do not go on television so that you can hide in the corner. But I saw myself more as the calm, cool, and collected type. To get ready for the show I thought at length about how I could stay true to myself, while still being engaging and entertaining. I eventually concluded that the best way to be engaging on the dates and on camera was to fully embrace who I am and to be completely vulnerable. I wanted the person on the other side of the wall to love and appreciate my true self, not my representative self. While I had always been confident in who I was, I ended this period of mental preparation more sure of myself than ever before.

I also invested time and energy into looking my best. I was hitting the gym more than I'd ever done before, while also whitening my teeth and working on my tan (hard to believe, I know, since I still came off as pretty pale under the harsh studio lights!). I upgraded my wardrobe too. These might sound like shallow pursuits, but like I said, I took the process seriously. At a certain point, I realized I was not simply trying to look my best for the show, I was relishing the opportunity to take better care of myself, without criticizing myself for being vain. Looks are not everything, but it is important to care for yourself and to feel confident in who you are.

Last but not least, I spent hours with my journal, thinking deeply about what I wanted in a partner and in a relationship. This is something else that I encourage everyone to do as a way of working through dating, especially if you have a history of dating the wrong type of people. It's easy to fall into the pattern of dating people who seem to be a good match on the surface but lack the qualities you need in a partner for long-term compatibility. You can break out of this pattern by thinking deliberately about the qualities that matter most to you and your absolute deal breakers for a relationship. Here are a few actual journal entries from that time:

- **Turnoffs:** someone who thinks they're better than others; infidelity (ask if they've ever cheated before); lack of empathy; bad hygiene; prejudice; does not think critically.
- **Turn-ons:** someone who is thoughtful; little reminders that show they care; empathy; faithful; someone who accepts all people; strong communicator; they're not afraid to nip a relationship problem in the bud before it gets out of hand.
- Focus on learning as much about the other person as possible, rather than talking about yourself. Make a conscious effort to listen and ask questions more than you talk. Try to ask questions beyond simple yes-or-no questions—ask open-ended questions.
- **Some questions to ask:** What's one of your biggest regrets? What are the biggest priorities in your life? Who are you closest to? What makes you happy? What's your idea of the perfect date? What's your current plan for achieving your goals?

I'm grateful that I took things seriously for the show. I believe people receive from life's opportunities what they put into them. Dating and relationships are no exception. I believe it was my commitment to being my best and being honest with myself about who I am and what I need that allowed me to find my soul mate.

chapter seven

ABOUT TO GET REAL

Hey, it's Lauren and Cameron here. We've been talking to you separately so far in the book because our stories up until this point have been our own, the paths that led us to *Love Is Blind*. But now that the story is about to enter our shared experience on the show, we're going to start to tell it as one. As you heard in the preface, we wanted to write this book to share the details of our extraordinary love story but also to impart some of the best relationship advice that we've gathered along the way. It's easier to do that if we're talking together.

We don't pretend to have all the answers about love and marriage. But we feel like the process of coming together in the pressure cooker setting of *Love Is Blind* gave us many unique insights into what works and what doesn't in a relationship. As we like to say, it felt like we packed a year into the seven weeks of the *Love Is Blind* experiment. And the journey since then hasn't slowed down.

Okay then, back to the story, beginning with the long-awaited arrival on the set of *Love Is Blind*.

Lauren

So, as you know, I found out that I made the cut for the show three days before taping was scheduled to begin (according to one of the producers, this was due to a delay with my background check, though who knows, it may well be that another girl dropped out last minute). And oh yeah, I was still in Europe at the time! You could say my preparations were a whirlwind. Unlike Cameron, I didn't start preparing months in advance. I arrived back in Atlanta from Paris late Saturday, so I basically had one day to pack, not to mention fill my parents in on the news. My dad was still like, "Baby, this is crazy." And my mom was still like, "Well, hey, go out there and find yourself a husband!"

Honestly, I was thinking more about the other girls during that mad thirty-six-hour sprint. Were they going to be mean and catty? I'd never been on a reality show, but I'd seen enough of them to know not everyone is the kind, caring type. Mentally preparing for all that in less than two days was insane. A year earlier I had been battling depression and crying fits. It's amazing how much your life can change so quickly. It goes to show that life is filled with ups and downs, and that it's worth fighting through even the lowest of lows.

As for my actual packing, the producers didn't offer too much guidance. They told us to bring different options—outfits we'd wear on dates but also beach clothes and comfy attire like sweatpants and pajamas. I'd later learn that a lot of the girls had hired stylists and personal shoppers to help them assemble the perfect looks, down to the last accessory. They were like Cameron times a hundred with their prep work! Jessica Batten, the blond-haired, blue-eyed beauty who would be at the center of the show's thorniest love triangle, even talked about having a friend who owned a clothing boutique and hooked her up with a full wardrobe. Meanwhile, I was raiding my closet, grabbing whatever I could find. I know what colors look good on my skin, luckily, so a lot of bright greens and oranges made it into the suitcase. I was also sure to pack my killer dresses: the really cute, formfitting numbers. My boobs are my secret weapons. Like I always say, they won't look this way forever!

Cameron

Because I got the news that I was officially cast a few weeks before filming, my experience wasn't quite the mad dash that Lauren went through. I'm not sure why they let me know so much earlier than Lauren—it probably had something to do with the fact that I was constantly checking in with the producer to see if there were any updates. I had been preparing since the start of the casting process, but once I got the official green light it was all systems go. A small part of me was still worried that I'd be dropped at the last minute, which apparently did end up happening to some people. That would have been devastating for me. But the producer was very reassuring. "You've got nothing to worry about; you're good to go," he'd say. "Just go out there and be yourself."

It was difficult to tell my parents that I was going on the show when I had denied how serious I was about the opportunity over the last few months. My mom still wasn't happy. A few days before departure, she called and sounded more serious than I'd ever heard her sound.

"I'm just worried about you getting humiliated or getting your heart broken. You know they can edit you to make it look like you said something you didn't," she said.

"I appreciate your concern, Mom," I told her. "I understand that they can edit me to look a certain way, but I feel like if I stay true to myself, then they'll have a harder time painting me in a bad light."

"I suppose that's true," she allowed.

"And besides, Mom," I added, "it's not like I'm actually going to get married there. It's just going to be a fun, two-week adventure."

The feeling of destiny about the show truly had intensified for me. I knew in my heart that whatever forces were guiding me were leading me in the right direction.

Lauren

I reached a moment, too, where I was just like, *Okay, God, it's in your hands now.* But I don't think I was as calm as Cameron, definitely not that Monday morning when I left my apartment for the set. They picked me up in an Uber and took me to this hotel outside Atlanta. It was an older-looking building, with not much else around it. I remember thinking to myself, *Oh Lord, what have I gotten myself into!* I admit I might have been a little paranoid, although I knew at this point that Netflix was behind the production.

But as I walked inside, I saw a bunch of other girls along with some producer types. That set my mind at ease. They were going to take our phones away for good at that point, so I snuck into the bathroom and texted my parents. "I'm here," I wrote. "It seems to be legit." But as I went to sleep later that night, I still wasn't sure.

Cameron

It was intense arriving at the hotel. I knew as soon as I walked inside it was go time. As I entered the hotel, I was brought into a drab conference room. A bunch of the other guys were already there, and more soon filtered in. They were getting rowdy, telling stories and boasting about their exploits. The level of posturing in the room was rising higher and higher—guys were talking over one another and were trying to tell the tallest tale. I just sat back and tried to take it all in. I remember thinking, *Okay, these are your typical reality TV bros.*

There was an ungodly amount of paperwork to fill out. That included W-2 forms, because we were getting paid to be on the show. That's something people always ask about. By law, you do have to get paid for reality television, but when you add up all the time you're on camera—sixteen hours a day sometimes—it's definitely lower than minimum wage. So nobody is getting rich.

At one point, one of the producers came in and said, "Okay, guys, it's time to get fitted for your wedding ring." I looked up from my conversation with one of the guys to see a producer approaching me with a set of plastic rings of different sizes. My heart started racing as the stakes of this experiment were more tangible than ever before. My hand had the slightest shake as she slipped on the first ring. "Nope, too small," she said. She put a bigger ring on my finger. "There we go, perfect." I looked down at the plastic ring on my finger and, for a moment, considered that there was the slightest chance I might come out of this wearing one for real.

It was a lot of hurry up and wait that first day, which was reminiscent of my firefighting days—long stretches of boredom broken up by bursts of intensity. Everyone in the room seemed to be huddled into small groups in their own conversations. I remember one guy starting up a conversation with me while we were waiting for the ring fitting. He started asking me questions about the kind of women I'm into.

"Do you like Black women?" he asked. He himself was a Black man.

"Yeah, of course," I answered.

"Well, I'm sorry to tell you, but you and I aren't going to be competing for the same women here."

"Why's that?" I asked.

"Black women won't be interested in you," he said.

"I mean, I've dated Black women in the past, so I don't think it will be a problem."

"Oh really?" he replied, sounding genuinely surprised.

"Yeah, man. I'm open to dating women from all different backgrounds, but admittedly I do find myself attracted to Black women more often. But I suppose since we won't be able to see the women on the other side of the wall, none of that matters anyway."

"Yeah, I guess you're right," he replied with a chuckle.

Lauren

Over on the girls' side, I was actually surprised that everyone was so friendly and nice. LC—Lauren Chamblin—was one of the first girls I met. "Oh my God, my name's Lauren too!" she said warmly. Kelly looked like she just walked off a canoe trip, real earthy and au naturel. Jessica had the Valley Girl thing going full tilt, while Gigi had more of a Kylie Jenner vibe. As for Amber, I remember her walking around that first day with this huge military bag and some kind of cast on her foot from an injury she'd gotten while working. I was like, *Who is this chick? What the hell?!* She was crazy from the jump!

But none of the girls seemed catty or overly competitive. We all kind of banded together, maybe because it still felt a little scary. The fear only intensified the next morning when they piled us all into a van with black garbage bags taped to the windows. This was part of the ongoing effort to keep our location top secret, and it was also to make absolutely certain that we wouldn't see the guys, say if our van happened to stop next to theirs at a traffic light or if we passed each other on the highway.

"Okay, this is creepy as hell," I said to a murmur of agreement from the other ladies as I boarded the van. But then we made it to the studio—Pinewood Atlanta Studios, which is where *Avengers: Endgame* was shot, along with a bunch of other blockbuster movies and shows. One of the girls even said she saw Robert Downey Jr. walking around with a few other stars. I remember being in a state of shock, thinking to myself, *Wow, this is for real. I am definitely on a* real *reality show.*

Cameron

I was ready to go when I woke up. I put on my blue suit with the red tie, which I'd ironed the night before, and took a few minutes to meditate on what lay ahead of me before heading to the lobby. The hotel had breakfast for us, but I couldn't really eat and a lot of the guys were the same way. Everyone was charged up. We were herded into a couple vans, also with those blacked-out windows.

Guys started telling more war stories, again with a lot of bravado. Mark and Damian both told stories about bar fights where they had helped out a friend who was being harassed. Many of the guys talked about the casual or complicated relationship they had ended so they could participate in this experiment. Despite all the one-upmanship, the comradery was strong from the start, I think due to how foreign and exciting this was to all of us.

When we reached the studio, I marveled at how massive the sound stages were. At ours, we were told to wait out in the parking lot until further instructions. The ninety-degree Georgia heat and humidity was making me rethink the suit. I talked a bit more to Barnett, whom I remembered from my psychiatry evaluation a couple months earlier. He was more personable than that snarky comment had let on! I realized there was more to him than my first impression. Kenny seemed like a good guy—he was a smooth talker from the jump, in that he was laser focused on the conversation when I talked to him and his southern drawl seemed friendly. I didn't get much of a chance to talk to Mark at first, but what I observed was that he could make friends with anyone. Damian wanted to bond over the fact that we both had red beards. From the start, he struck me as larger than life, as he, at first, was usually the loudest in the room or the one doing stunts like mixing coffee grounds with peanut butter and eating it. I quickly learned that he is a very sensitive and thoughtful person, though, and I could tell that he was going to be someone who stood out from the crowd. Carlton seemed shy and demure initially. I thought there wouldn't be a lot of drama there—clearly an egregious error in judgment on my part!

Finally, the producers told us they were ready for us. They walked us to the very edge of the sound stage, where we were getting mic'd up before the cameras finally started rolling. My nerves were firing on all cylinders. Barnett and I chatted some more as the line inched forward. He told me how nervous he was feeling.

"Yeah, me too," I said.

"No, dude, I'm about to shit my pants right now," he added with a mischievous yet anxious grin.

"Okay, well, don't do that," I replied.

They were sending us in one by one onto the sound stage. Each time, as the door opened and closed, I was able to catch a glimpse of the set. It looked completely surreal, a blue-lit artificial world that I was about to be transported to.

"Cameron, you're up," the producer said.

I thought back to all the preparation that had led up to this and whispered to myself, "It's go time."

Part II

chapter eight

YOUR REAL SELF

Cameron

As I made my way onto the set of *Love Is Blind*, I felt like I was entering another world. The layout of the men's facility was surreal yet strangely familiar, like a cross between an upscale frat house and a model home. I can still picture it perfectly in my mind— the oversize armchairs, the towering bar packed to the gills with liquor, the television built into the wall with an animated fire burning 24/7, and the slightly lopsided pool table that was apparently built by the set designers. "Wouldn't it have been easier just to buy a pool table?" I mused to one of the guys while playing a game before the first dates started.

Then there was the small gym off the kitchen. While anxiously awaiting the start of the dates, Damian and I decided to blow off some steam by lifting weights. The bench press collapsed when I sat on it! It turned out the crew hadn't screwed the bench to the rest of the frame. The surrealness came from realizing that some things were real, some things were not, and some things, like the pool table, were somewhere in between. Everything was just a little bit off. I wondered how it would be possible to have genuine feelings and emotions while surrounded by so much artifice. *Welcome to reality TV*, I told myself.

While surveying the men's lounge, I remembered some of my mom's parting advice: "Don't forget about the Stanford Prison Experiment!" If you're unfamiliar, the Stanford Prison Experiment was a controversial psychology experiment conducted in the 1970s where the student participants were randomly divided into prisoners and guards and placed into a mock prison setup in the basement of Stanford's psychology department. The students were each told to assume the role they were assigned but were not given much further instruction. At first, the students didn't take their roles seriously, but after six days the experiment had to be shut down, as they had all conformed to their roles too well. They could no longer distinguish the experiment from reality. "I won't forget, Mom." As I looked around at the rest of the guys pouring drinks and conversing, I wondered how those students at Stanford felt as they entered the basement of the psychology department for the first time.

And there were cameras *everywhere*—something like four hundred in all throughout the entire sound stage, including in the lounge area, the gym, the kitchen, and the main hallway leading to the pods and of course all over the pods themselves. There were cameras embedded into the walls, over the doorways, and mounted to a steel grid that hung ominously overhead. On several dates, I would look up to see one of these overhead cameras looking down on me before it whizzed off to another pod. The on-camera conversations were a bit stiff at first, but everyone loosened up quickly enough. The posturing started once everyone got comfortable with the cameras. There were many times when I'd be having a normal conversation with one of the guys, and suddenly he would switch into a dramatic and seemingly prepared monologue as he noticed the cameras approaching. I wasn't about to jockey for the spotlight, so I listened and observed, staying focused on why I was there in the first place: the prospect of finding true love.

Lauren

It was a similar scene on the girls' side. They walked us into the main lounge area, sat us down, and everyone was super nervous, like, *Oh. My. God. We're really doing this!* But very quickly, the personalities with some of the girls switched from shy and demure to really wanting to be seen, fluffing themselves up, looking to grab more camera time. Acting as their *representative*—a persona based on who they really are—it's just that little . . . extra, you know? The show's set was a microscope, so everything was amplified, including this notion of the representative. There were many times that first day when I found myself thinking, *I've never heard so many story-speeches or seen so many random outpourings of tears.*

I mean, I get it . . . the hot lights of the cameras can be a bit much. Working as a model, I'm aware of the fact that many people cringe or shy away when someone whips a camera out, but there are also those who can flip that "on" switch and come alive. I have such a strong personality, it's hard for me to NOT be myself. I've never felt the pull to preen, regardless of the situation, even if there are a few hundred cameras capturing my every move.

Throughout the entire *LIB* process, from the very first Skype interview, there was never a moment where I felt like I had to get into character. Whether it was being chosen to be on the show in the first place or going on to find a husband, I wanted the outcome to be truly reflective of me. And so I was always honest about the things I said. I never tried to become someone or something I'm not. In social situations: if a good-looking guy walks into a room, some might fluff themselves up or laugh a little bit louder to make sure they're being seen. The problem is, it becomes impossible to keep up the act forever—including in relationships. I wasn't going to fall into that trap—not in real life and definitely not on the show. It was important to be myself in my purest form: raw, vulnerable, real, transparent, and 100 percent *me*.

Cameron

After hours of speculating what the pods would be like and who the women were on the other side of the wall, we got word from the producers that it was time to enter the pods. When I heard my name in the roster, I lined up behind the rest of the guys. I felt an immense rush as I entered the center hallway that divided the men's facility and the pods, with its row of ten doors leading into the ten pods. I took my place in front of my door and began rocking back and forth on the balls of my feet while I tried to focus myself on being present for the impending date. Guys were doing everything they could to psych themselves up. Mark had this funny chant that he repeated over and over: "One time for the one time, I'm here for a good time, not a long time."

"Aren't we looking for someone for a long time?" I shouted to him across the hallway.

"It is what it is, bro!" he shouted back.

"That doesn't make sense either."

"It doesn't need to!"

Whatever gets you psyched up to enter the pods, right?

The producers kept us penned up in the hallway for a solid fifteen minutes, which after the months of anticipation felt like an eternity. Finally, the loudspeaker crackled to life and an anonymous voice announced, "You may now enter the pods." I cautiously pushed the door open and stepped inside. It was a cozy octagonal space, with insulated walls (for the acoustics, I believe), a couch, blankets, and a small side table stocked with mini bottles of booze and candy. A hypnotic blue screen filled the wall in front of the couch.

"Hello? . . . Hello?" I said as I entered the pod. At first, there was no response. But ten seconds later, I heard the door on the other side of the blue screen open and close.

"Hello?" a woman's voice said.

"Hi, I'm Cameron."

"Hi! I'm Diamond."

She was friendly and personable, right off the bat. As we began to commiserate about how surreal and exciting this all was, my anxiety started to fade. It began feeling like we were on a date, despite being separated by a glowing hypnotic wall. We had an instant rapport, which started as flirtatious, then evolved to friendly and platonic over the nine days that followed. When she told me she was a dancer for the NBA, I was expecting her to be more performative, but she was humble and down to earth. After we said our good-byes, I walked out of the pod feeling like there might be a glimmer of hope that I could connect with someone here.

That was not the case with many of the dates that followed. I was able to eliminate several women right out of the gate because they talked about themselves for the entire ten minutes. The dates literally consisted of one continuous monologue. I might as well not even have been there. Not that I needed to do all the talking, but I think it's important in a relationship for there to be give and take—for your partner to have a genuine curiosity about you, and you about them.

After my ninth date that day, I found myself overwhelmed trying to mentally sort all the women and what I had learned about them. Some were memorable, like Diamond, while others were hard to place. Still, I wasn't sure if I had *really* connected yet, even if the dates were feeling more real than I had anticipated. Eager for my next date, I approached the producer standing in front of the door leading to the hallway.

"Can you tell me who's my next date with?"

"Hmm . . . let's see," he replied, looking down at the sheet of paper he was holding. "Looks like your next date is with . . . Lauren."

As we said our hellos, I could tell there was something different about this date, something electric.

"Where are you from, Cameron?" she asked warmly.

"I'm from the state of Maine," I responded, a big smile on my face.

"I've never met anyone from Maine," she said.

"Well, I'm the only one you'll ever need to meet," I answered, matching her playfulness.

I could feel the sparks already igniting. From the intonation of Lauren's laugh, I could sense her incredible spirit. It was love at first laugh, you might say. As we continued talking, I felt I could trust her. She made me feel both comfortable and at the edge of my seat at the same time.

"So, what is it that really drives you?" I asked her toward the end of that first date.

"I have a creative vision I want to turn into a reality. I own my own business, The Speed Brand, and I have so many stories I want to tell about myself, my family, where I'm from, and other narratives I've come up with. I come from an entertainment family and I want to do more projects with them."

"That's a beautiful thing to be able to work with your family. And I must say I have an immense amount of respect for people who run their own business."

"So, what about you?"

"Well, besides taking over the world, I want to use AI to help make the world a better place. I have some ideas about how AI can be used to help improve diagnosis and treatment of disease and also how it can be applied in people's day-to-day lives."

"Wow, I would love to hear more about that."

"Thirty seconds remaining," announced a voice over the pod's intercom. "Please wrap up your date." Ten minutes had flown by in what seemed like moments. I felt a pang of disappointment as we said our good-byes. Now the experiment felt like a tease. Here we were starting to kindle our initial sparks, yet Production had all these rules about how long the dates were and whom we went on dates with. I didn't want to go on the remaining five dates I had that day; I wanted to get to know Lauren more. Nevertheless, as I stepped into the bright light of the hallway I was grinning ear to ear.

Lauren

That first date with Cameron was on a different level. I felt a few sparks with some of the other guys, but it was purely flirtatious fun. Damian and I had a few pleasant dates, but as with Cam and Diamond, the relationship pretty quickly settled on platonic ground. I also got along well with Matt—not Matt Barnett, the *other* Matt, or Boxer Matt as we called him because he ran a boxing gym. We had interesting discussions about the nature of love and relationships. But after a few dates, as my feelings for Cam deepened, it turned into this therapist/client dynamic with Boxer Matt where he would ask questions to get into my head as a way to understand the *LIB* experiment that we were both going through. It became a little strange, though not to the extent of some of my other dates. Let me tell you, there were some odd characters in the mix. Those casting agents knew what they were doing!

I remember one guy saying, within the first minute of the first date, "Are you Black? Because you sound Black."

"No, I'm white," I responded, just to mess with his head a little. I mean, the whole point of the show was to not focus on appearances! *Hello!!!*

I also remember talking to Carlton for the first time. So many of the girls were crazy about Carlton. "Ooh, he's so smooth," they said. "He's so *this*. He's so *that*." For me, after our first date I was like, *Nah, it's just not clicking for me.* He was *too* smooth.

With a lot of the guys, I had this sense that they were trying to hide something. They would drone on and on about their career accomplishments or they would take the opposite approach and pretend to be extra sensitive and self-aware. In both cases, it felt like not everyone was being honest about who they really were. They thought they were impressing me. Nope! I was bored!

This disconnect is something I'd seen so much during my dating life in the outside world. People are so afraid to be themselves. So they fall back on their representative, that persona they present when first meeting someone because they believe it will impress. They're afraid that if they reveal their true self right away, it will scare the other person off. That's such a crazy thought process. Why are you afraid to be yourself with someone you're considering dating or possibly marrying—even having kids with? Or having sex with? Why, as a society, are people so afraid to be themselves and to be judged? Not to mention loved?

Cameron was just the opposite. During our first date, I felt his honesty and warmth. He shared with me intimate details about his family, including the fact that his mom has Parkinson's and how that's something he struggles with, wanting to do more to keep her healthy. And he talked about his ambitions as a scientist. There was also a playfulness to him that I found very comforting.

Cameron

It was easy to keep it playful with Lauren while also having serious discussions because there was no artifice between us: I could tell she was being genuine with me by the way she opened up about the difficulties she had experienced in her life such as her parents' divorce and having been cheated on in a past relationship. I, too, had been cheated on in the past, but I only felt comfortable talking to Lauren about it. I talked to her about my mom's health concerns and my feeling responsible for finding a solution to them.

Lauren and I also talked about our lifestyles. I was transparent about the fact that my career and my family are my main focus in life and that I didn't spend a lot of time going out or socializing. We bonded over both being self-proclaimed hermits, while still appreciating the chance to go on an adventure. On dates with other women in the pods, I got the sense they were looking for guys with particular traits and lifestyle choices. On dates with Jessica and Amber, for example, I could tell they were interested in guys who are into sports. On dates with Brianna and some of the other women, they expressed a desire for a man with particular religious beliefs. Some women wanted a partner who was down to party and who was also the life of the party. In each one of these dates, I let these women know the truth about who I am. While this led to a sudden mutual understanding that most of these dates weren't going anywhere, Lauren accepted me for me. I wasn't about to feign interest in something or someone and I didn't need to. I had met someone who was truly interested in me for me, not who she wanted me to be, and I was falling for her.

We all have unique personalities. I've always believed that one of my defining characteristics is a willingness to show emotion, and I view that as a strength. When you allow yourself to be vulnerable, you are opening yourself up for the other person to reject you or put you down in some way. But if you have the inner confidence to take that chance and you end up finding a person who accepts you, then the relationship begins on a foundation of support and empathy, potentially leading to a deep and meaningful love.

Lauren and I shared that willingness to be vulnerable from the very beginning. We were able to find the balance between keeping it fun and flirtatious while also asking each other the serious questions we knew we needed to ask: "What are your career goals?" "How do you feel about raising children?" "What do you truly believe in?" "What are your biggest fears?" "What's something you have done that you're really proud of?" "What's something you've done you aren't proud of?" "Why do you think your past relationships didn't work out?" "What do you feel like you need in life to be truly happy?"

Conventional wisdom cautions us not to get too serious too fast, like it's somehow wrong to show genuine interest in the other person, whether it's by asking them earnest questions or responding too quickly to their texts. I could tell right away that Lauren, like me, wasn't into that kind of game-playing. Our connection felt fated from the first date, and that feeling strengthened with each conversation that followed. Our chemistry grew exponentially because of how vulnerable we were willing to be with each other. Not a minute in the pods was wasted.

I'll admit this was all a little terrifying, as I had to concede to the possibility that the woman I was starting to fall for might not conform to my conception of beauty. During later dates with other women, I would sometimes ask what Lauren looked like, but I only ever got vague descriptions. "She's very graceful," they'd say. Or "she carries herself well." None of them ever told me how stunning she is, maybe because they were trying to maintain a competitive edge. We were all technically dating each other, after all! Regardless, I was becoming so enamored with Lauren that I told myself we would be able to work through it if the physical chemistry wasn't there. Fortunately, we never had to put that theory to the test. I knew my feelings for Lauren were worth taking a leap of faith, without knowing what awaited me when I landed. Falling in love sight unseen is not for the faint of heart.

Lauren

With Cameron and *Love Is Blind*, that's the first time I felt the spark go off without anything physical. Usually there's at least a picture on Instagram. But in this case, there was just this voice on the other side of the wall. That was kind of liberating. Because, let's face it, physical appearances can complicate dating. Maybe you don't really feel any spark, but you keep dating the person because they're attractive. You say to yourself, "I'm not really into this person, but maybe it will change; maybe the chemistry will grow." Then you end up in a relationship with no emotional or intellectual core.

It's even worse in the age of dating apps, which are almost entirely based on what people look like. You see someone attractive who you want to pursue, and you simply double tap or swipe right. And on other social media apps, like Instagram and Facebook, we tend to buy into attractive, shiny, beautiful pictures. We're less inclined to think, *I really like this person's personality!*

Love Is Blind took away all those surface-level things—the physical contact and attraction, the first kiss, the sex. It was dating based purely on conversation and connection. If you didn't feel the connection, you moved on. There would probably be a lot fewer hearts broken and years lost to dead-end relationships if the same thing happened in the real world.

Cameron

Though to be clear, not everyone on the show was having the same experience as Lauren and me. On day three, I returned to the men's lounge from a date and noticed that half the guys were missing. Those of us who remained started nervously chatting, asking if anyone knew what was going on. A few minutes later, the executive producers came into the lounge.

"As I'm sure you've noticed, some of the guys are no longer in the facility with us," one of the producers said. "The fact is, they weren't making connections, so we decided to send them home. The good news is that this will give you all more time to concentrate on the people on the other side of the wall who you are building connections with."

There was a collective panic building among the remaining men. Production had not mentioned anything about people being sent home until that day. Everyone was looking wide-eyed at each other, likely calculating whether they were next to be eliminated. While I had considered the possibility that some of us would be cut, it was another thing entirely to have this speculation confirmed. Despite the uneasiness in the air, I felt a strange sense of calm. Lauren and I had already formed a strong connection and I knew the producers had recognized that as well. It was also becoming more and more apparent who Production was interested in by how much camera time they received. It seemed the cameras were constantly focused on Damian, Mark, Kenny, Barnett, Carlton, and me.

Still, later that night I heeded the advice of the producers and went back to my room to do some serious reflecting in my journal. I had my mom's voice in my head saying, *Don't get caught up in the glamour of the show and the romance of it all.* My mind kept coming back to Lauren. I played devil's advocate with myself, racking my brain for possible red flags to make absolutely certain that I wasn't mistaking the whirlwind experience of the show for romance. I couldn't come up with any warning signs, but I did jot down some more questions I felt were important tests of true compatibility:

- *If we were to get into a heated argument, how do you think we should resolve it?*
- *If we were in a relationship, how should we balance the time we spend together and the time we spend individually?*
- *What would we do if one of us got a dream job offer in a different state/country? Would we move together or make long distance work?*
- *If we had kids, how would you want to discipline our children?*
- *How should we manage our finances if one of us is making significantly more than the other?*

Some couples will be in a relationship for years without knowing how their partner feels about having kids, managing finances, or even sharing responsibilities in the household. In the three short dates Lauren and I had had, I learned how she felt about all those things, and so much more. I couldn't wait to get back into the pod and learn more.

The Dos and Don'ts of First Dates

First dates aren't easy. For many people, they're downright terrifying. Keep in mind that the other person is probably feeling just as uncomfortable as you are. Moments of not knowing what to talk about are par for the course with first dates, so don't stress if there are some lulls in the conversation. Once you get past the initial jitters, it is usually smooth sailing. However, it never hurts to brainstorm some questions or conversation starters you'd like to discuss before the date starts.

Now that we've walked you through our first date, here are some words of wisdom on the subject, based on our experiences:

Do be yourself. Authenticity is the most important quality you can bring to a relationship, and the tone is set on the first date. Showing a little vulnerability is the best way to bring truth and honest emotion into the conversation. It can be difficult to be open about your past mistakes, your ambitions for the future, your fears, and what means the most to you, but this type of sharing is what endears you to others. You will have to use your best judgment to decide how much to share and how fast, but there is always an inherent risk the other person will not be sensitive to your vulnerability. If they are able to relate to what you share and show compassion, however, you will have started a connection.

Do listen. Monologuing during a first date is the kiss of death. For some people, it's just a nervous reflex. Having a go-to list of questions will help you remember to take a breath and turn the conversation back to the other person.

Do reflect later. Whether you thought the date was amazing, horrible, or somewhere in the middle, take a few minutes later that night or the following morning to truly reflect on the experience. Even if you decide to never see the person again, this exercise in reflection will help you understand what you're looking for in a partner and in a relationship.

Don't get hung up on appearances. Look, we get it—physical attraction is real and it would be misleading to say that looks don't matter at all. There has to be some baseline of mutual physical attraction for the relationship to work long-term. But if a person's sexy body or beautiful face is literally the only thing you're into about them, you have to find a way to move on. A relationship built only on physical attraction will go nowhere fast!

Don't fall for the idea of a person. Maybe you think you have to be with a doctor or a model or an athlete. Maybe your potential partner has to make a lot of money or have thousands of followers on social media. Too many people judge potential partners by what they do instead of who they are. Don't fall into that trap. Just as you need to be completely authentic when it comes to matters of the heart, instead of falling back on your representative self, it's important to see potential partners for who they really are, and not for who you want them to be.

Don't ignore your gut. First impressions are usually pretty accurate. If you feel like something is off about the person or the chemistry between you, do not ignore this feeling. That doesn't mean that you should look for reasons to dismiss the person you are dating, but you should trust those visceral feelings that tell you the other person is ultimately not right for you.

chapter nine

CITY GIRL, COUNTRY BOY

Lauren

When I was a kid, my dad used to take my brother and me on these great adventures into downtown Detroit. We'd bundle up and head for the bus stop, running by the convenience store to stock up on snacks for the ride. I always got the same combo—a bag of Cheetos, an orange-flavored Faygo pop, and a pack of Now and Laters. We'd climb on board, grab our seats, and make our way to Cadillac Square, down by the river, where we'd watch the pigeons and admire the various street performers, including the guys playing bongos with a set of upside-down paint cans.

Today, anytime I'm coming home and I see the GM building, which really defined the downtown skyline when I was young, I feel that swell of hometown pride. Detroit has a hustler spirit like nothing else I've ever experienced. The hardworking, blue-collar mentality is deeply ingrained. And with all the factories, the sight of smog and the smell of exhaust is seared into my memory.

Remember, Detroit is where the car was born! But there's so much other beauty to go along—the history, the art, the culture, and of course the music, starting with Motown and continuing today with so many amazing artists, from Big Sean to Eminem.

That's what those early adventures with my dad taught me, that Detroit is a special place where people find joy no matter how hard or gritty things might appear to the outside world. We always make the most of what we have. That fighting spirit is a huge part of my identity.

When I first met Cameron and he told me he was from a super small town in Maine with a population of eight hundred, I thought, *Detroit and Maine? Two completely different worlds.* It would have been easy to say, "Next contestant! Because there's no way this one is gonna work."

I'm glad I shut that thought down. Dating someone from a different background shouldn't be scary or intimidating. Just the opposite, it's a chance for both partners to learn new things and expand as people.

Cameron

Yes, Lauren and I discovered on our early dates that, despite our outward differences, we had so many more things in common than apart, including how we were raised and the family values we share. We were both taught the importance of hard work from an early age. I had my first job at the age of thirteen, raking blueberries at a local farm. Then there were all the summers in high school working as a caretaker at a local beach, mowing lawns and painting picnic tables. Lauren laughed at my stories of working as a barista at a Cuban café in grad school, when I used to hide in the kitchen anytime one of my students came in for a drink (some of my students stalked me but that's a story for another time). And, of course, I was proud to recount my experiences fighting wildfires from coast to coast.

Lauren

Not to be outdone, I told Cam about my time working as a bank teller when I was a college freshman. We're both overachievers, so there was definitely a playful comparison going on. I shared stories about collecting urine samples at a medical clinic when I was desperate for a job after college and some of the salacious details from my work as a bartender in Detroit, when it was common to see politicians out cavorting with their mistresses. And I delved into my various jobs in entertainment, first a model, then a DJ, then the host of my own show on public access television, *The Elle Speed Show*. While we were having fun sharing stories of our colorful work history, we were strengthening our bond over our core values of hard work and individualism.

The more we talked, the more common ground we found. For example, I was very into art and acting growing up, a true theater geek. It turned out Cam was the same way. I loved hearing that he even went to musical theater camp during the summer as a kid. It was a real "No way, same with me!" moment. We definitely match geekiness when it comes to theater and creativity. Which was great to discover, because I've always believed that people who are creative are in touch with their inner child, since that's where the imagination stems from for most creatives.

Another example: Cam described his family as being well known throughout town, real pillars of the community. It reminded me so much of my family's role in our neighborhood in Detroit. When I was growing up, my next-door neighbor and childhood bestie was a girl named Jennifer. One day, a group of girls from school followed her home, looking to pick a fight. My dad tore out of the house, broke up the fight, and made sure Jennifer got home safely. My father was a lot like Laurence Fishburne's character in *Boyz n the Hood*. He was my dad, but at times he was a father figure to a lot of others in our community. And I could tell it was the same way growing up a Hamilton in rural Maine.

Cameron

I think many people make the mistake of thinking that if someone is from a different background then they can't be compatible. This is a limiting belief. Many people put constraints on their own happiness and success by believing they are incapable of something that may require stepping out of their comfort zone or going against what they've been told by others.

I've always taken the view that differences in a relationship can be complementary if both people are willing to work together. If you are fortunate, you can find someone who has strengths where you have weaknesses. For example, Lauren has taught me about how to pose for pictures, how to light the set, and how to frame a shot. I have taught her about investing and the stock market. She has educated me on Black culture and what it was like to grow up in Detroit. I showed her Maine culture and how rewarding it can be to spend more time in nature. She has taught me to feel more comfortable dancing, and I have taught her to feel more comfortable cooking. I believe the best partner is someone who can challenge you and teach you things that help you grow.

Lauren

That's true even when the difference is as evident as racial background. That's a whole conversation in and of itself, and it's one Cameron and I will tackle head on in a later chapter. But to pick up on what Cam was saying, it helps to think of dating someone different as both a teaching and a learning opportunity. I'll teach you something about my world, you'll teach me something about yours, and together we'll grow as people. That was the understanding we reached from the very beginning in the pods and it continues to this day.

I remember the first time I went to visit Cam's family in Maine. They had a lot of customs and traditions that were alien to me. I swear, the number of times I thought to myself, *This is DIFFERENT! We don't do this where I'm from.* A lot of the differences revolved around food. Like one night his parents put out these mincemeat pies, which I believe to be a New England thing. In my mind I'm thinking, *Ugh, fruit and red meat? No thank you, I will not be partaking in that.* And, yes, the whole oneness-with-nature vibe was a little jarring at first for this city girl. I'll never forget how deer in the yard would waltz right up to the kitchen window at the back of the house and sniff around. Cameron's dad would even leave apples for them to eat. Growing up in Detroit, that is *not* something I experienced often or even at all.

But you know, we had a good laugh over the situation, and it was fine. That's an important point to stress. Being with someone from a different background doesn't mean you have to become that person in every way, at the expense of your own identity and history. You just have to be open and interested in learning about them and sharing about yourself. Out of your two life experiences, a broader, deeper, richer union will form.

Cameron

Of course, this isn't to say that two people with very similar backgrounds cannot have a successful relationship. Look at Amber and Barnett. They were both raised in the South in families with similarly conservative leanings, and they're married and going strong. And there are plenty of happy couples who come from the same town or social circle. My parents, for example, grew up just a few towns apart and are now going on thirty-eight successful years of marriage. My dad started in the Maine Forest Service (MFS) as a laborer and worked his way to the very top as the director and chief forest ranger. A few years later, in the summer between high school and college, my mom got a laborer's job at the MFS working with my godmother, my mom's best friend, who was a campsite ranger. They managed campsites, painted picnic tables, operated a fire tower, and wore the Smokey the Bear costume for fairs and parades. My mom likes to say that's when she met that young handsome forest ranger.

But there is something to be said about the potential danger of relying too much on the convenient or comfortable. To be clear, there is absolutely nothing wrong with sharing a background with your partner and bonding over your similar upbringing. It is a wonderful thing to be able to relate to the people you care about on as many levels as possible. Bonding on a shared background is only problematic if that is the only level on which you and your partner can relate. It's disheartening to see couples whose initial bond formed based on their shared background fizzle out because they found out they were incompatible across other domains: values, life goals, marriage, children, finances, among others. Many partners fall into this trap. They take the path of least resistance, pairing off with someone from their close circle of friends or maybe their church or gym. There's nothing wrong with coupling up with someone close to home, but you still have to put in the work to get to know the other person on a deep level in order to understand whether you add value to each other's lives or get in each other's way. In the end, I think that couples who work the best together are those who share mutual respect and core values but who also have enough differences to bring color, richness, and variety to the relationship. By day four of *Love Is Blind*, when I realized the extent to which Lauren and I shared so many core values and I was able to envision our lives together without reservation, I knew she was the one.

Putting on the Blinders in Real Life

There's the old saying "opposites attract," but the truth is that as humans, we tend to gravitate toward people who look like us or remind us of where we come from. There's comfort and security in the familiar. But as we talked about throughout this chapter, surface similarities don't automatically translate into deep-seated compatibility. So how can you borrow from the *LIB* playbook without actually throwing on a blindfold before every date?

For starters, be open to love both inside and outside the comfort zone. It's great to meet people at school or church or any area of your common social circle—it means you already share something in common. But if you're somewhere else, a bookstore, say, or out walking in the park, and someone catches your eye (maybe you're attracted to their confident manner or infectious laugh), don't be afraid to engage. Many people are terrified of this kind of cold open because they're afraid of being rejected by a stranger. You don't have to ask them out on a date or for their phone number, at least not right away. Try a low-risk opener, like asking them for directions. Remember, people like to be helpful! And in the brief exchange, you should be able to pick up on whether the interest is mutual or not. If you're getting positive feedback and you sense the conversation is winding down, take a chance by asking for their number or their social media handle. If they say they're not interested, at least you got some good practice in for when you meet the right person!

Once you're dating, be sure to ask values-based questions starting from the very beginning. Of course, you want to know where the other person is from and what kind of work they do as well. Dig deeper by finding out what they liked about where they grew up or why they decided to enter into their chosen career. If you are really interested in someone, you likely want to know everything about them. We are simply highlighting how important it is to concentrate on asking them the questions that get at the root of who they are and how they have handled different events in their life. The conversation that is light and fun will come naturally, while these penetrating questions may not. Ask them questions that address reservations or problems you experienced in past relationships: Have they ever been unfaithful? Why do they think their last relationship did not work out? What are some qualities they feel they need in a partner and why are they important? It's about getting to the "why" of the person instead of just the "what."

As you ask these more insightful questions, look for common ground, regardless of whether your backgrounds are very similar or very different. It is possible that despite differences in where you grew up or what your lifestyle is like, you have more common ground than you initially realize. The people who work the best together are individuals who share core values but who also balance out each other's strengths and weaknesses and help each other grow.

chapter ten

THE TWO-DRINK
MAXIMUM RULE

Cameron

Reality shows have a reputation for plying cast members with booze and rolling the cameras for the ensuing train wreck. That wasn't my experience on *Love Is Blind*, but the set wasn't bone-dry either. The truth, I'd say, was somewhere in the middle. One of the producers once overheard Lauren and me talking about champagne and within minutes two champagne flutes appeared before us. No one was forcing a drink into your hand, but it was always around if you wanted it. And there's something about free alcohol that makes it hard to pass up.

I remember back on the first day of filming, when Nick and Vanessa Lachey, the show's hosts, shot their opening segment with us. As soon as they left the set, one of the producers shouted, "Okay, boys, the bar is open!" It was like animals to the watering hole. There was a lot of nervous energy in the air, especially since we were about to enter the pods for the first time. Guys were doing shots, mixing drinks, and playing beer pong before we had our first dates. Many were looking for that liquid courage to carry them through. I sat back, sipped my cognac, and watched.

Some of the guys were kids in a candy shop. It was like they'd never seen alcohol before. And the bar was *stocked*—beer, wine, champagne, every kind of spirit imaginable. It's funny, because our lodgings the first few days were quite meager: we were sleeping in trailers behind the sound stage. Someone even said he saw a "Department of Corrections" stamp on his bed. The sleeping conditions didn't bother me, as they reminded me of the cots I often slept on as a firefighter. But when a few of the women complained about the presence of cockroaches in their trailer, Production upgraded us to a nearby hotel. I had laugh to myself when I saw how the budget was being spent. Production clearly had their priorities.

As we were approaching the last few rounds of dates on the first day, Production came in and shut the bar down in the middle of a particularly rowdy game of beer pong. They told us that while they wanted us to have a good time, they felt the level of intoxication was taking away from the quality of the dates. Some of the guys countered with, "But the girls are drunk too!" While I was making some friends on the guys' side, the antics made me all the more eager to get back into the pods.

Lauren

I wish I could say it was a tamer scene over on our side, but the girls were knocking back the drinks as well. I woke up early the second morning and came out into the living area and a few of them were already at it.

"Who needs a drink?" one of the ladies shouted.

I declined. "It's seven a.m.!" I said.

But I was definitely in the minority. Alcohol is a social lubricant and, like Cam said, there were a lot of nerves on set. The booze helped people relax and feel more comfortable. It helped them get out of their heads and eliminate some of their fears. I get it. And in moderation, alcohol can be a benign addition.

But as we all know, alcohol and emotions aren't the best combination. And there was so much raw emotion on the show. We were digging deeply into emotional wounds that happened in past relationships or with our families. The booze was like lighter fluid.

Even in college, I was the one who would look after everyone else. There was a lot of, "Okay, maybe you should slow down," or "I'm not cleaning puke out of my car, it's time to go."

So it wasn't hard for me to be moderate during production. And to be honest I just didn't want to be drunk on television saying things that could be misconstrued. Especially because there are no redos in reality TV; once it's out there it's out there FOREVER. A lot of the girls—and guys—didn't seem that concerned. I had guys coming into the pod and slurring their words. I remember thinking to myself, *These people are, like, fucked up!* And of course, the editors focused on these train wreck moments when they stitched together the final cut of the show. I'm thinking of Amber's drunken confessional during the bachelorette party episode. Did she have too much to drink that night? Yes. But that moment wasn't reflective of the whole Amber. Like I said, though, most cast members weren't thinking about the long-term consequences of their actions, including having a few too many in front of the cameras.

But not Cameron. That was another thing that set him apart. I could tell from the opening "hello" that he was 100 percent present. Relative sobriety definitely became another point of connection. We both wanted to be fully in it.

Cameron

As I've said before, coming into *Love Is Blind*, I wanted to be mentally clear and 100 percent focused on the dates. I told myself that if I was going to do this experiment, I was going to commit to it fully. I knew that getting drunk would take away from forming a connection with someone on the other side of the wall.

I am not against drinking entirely: most nights I'll have a beer or a cognac at the end of the day to unwind. But unlike Lauren, I haven't always practiced restraint. I didn't drink in high school, but in college there were plenty of nights when I had a few too many. I can think of several times I missed my chance to get to know someone I was interested in because I was too inebriated to have a proper conversation. While I was in grad school for philosophy, I continued to overindulge: most weekends were spent drinking and arguing with my peers. I admittedly have many fond memories of those times, but at a certain point I realized the partying was affecting my quality of life. I didn't like waking up feeling depleted. I also didn't like the extra weight I was packing on. So I made the decision to dial it back.

It was clear that drinking in moderation helped set me apart from the other *LIB* guys. On many dates, the women would tell me that most of the guys on their previous dates that day had been wasted. I think some of the guys picked up on the fact that I wasn't drinking as much and actually resented me for it, like I was somehow getting one over on them.

There was one guy in particular who was hitting the sauce extra hard—he liked to mix dirty martinis first thing in the morning. One afternoon he cornered me in the lounge area.

"Hey, bro, how many drinks have you had today?" he asked, as he slapped his hand down on my shoulder.

"Why are you checking how many drinks I've had?" I asked.

"I haven't seen you drink anything today," he said.

"Don't worry about it; I'm good," I assured him, while staring him down.

My glare caught him off guard. "I just wanted to make sure you were having a good time," he replied before slinking away.

The experience made me wonder if the pressure to drink on other reality shows comes as much from other contestants as it does from the producers.

In any event, I didn't have to deal with Mr. Dirty Martini for very long since he was one of the first to leave the show. Most of the heavy drinkers were in the first wave of departures. You can't be drunk all the time and expect to find love.

Lauren

That became clear to me on the show. As I said, there was a lot of analysis of past relationships happening with the girls. At one point, I talked to them about my experience with my college boyfriend. He admitted after we had broken up that he cheated on me while we were dating, and his excuse was that he had been drunk. As if somehow that made it okay. It doesn't work like that. A relationship is about trust, honesty, and authenticity. If you're drinking to the point where you're doing things and making choices that you wouldn't make if you were sober, that's not okay. "I was drunk" is not an excuse.

And as I alluded to earlier with the Amber scene, the cast had no say in the editing of the show. The story the show wanted to tell about each of us was entirely up to the producers. That being said, they couldn't craft a story out of thin air. If you were doing a lot of drinking, they couldn't turn you into a lush through the magic of editing.

I know alcohol is a big part of our culture. And I enjoy it myself from time to time. But it's so important to always be present, especially when you're first dating someone new. You want to be relaxed and comfortable, but you also want to make sure that you're being your true self and that you're seeing the other person for who they really are.

Maxims of the Two-Drink Max

Booze is everywhere in our society, and there's a ton of pressure to partake. Here are a few rules that we follow to keep things fun but under control:

Beware the open bar. Nothing is free in life, and that includes booze. Whether it's a time-share presentation, a business event, or a reality TV show, you need to be wary when someone provides you with free alcohol, because it probably means they want something from you. Even if not, say at a wedding, open bars can sometimes lead to more harm than good. Rotating nonalcoholic drinks, ideally water, into the mix will limit your booze intake and help you stay good and hydrated for the next day.

Steer clear of sloppy sex. Hooking up under the influence can seem like a good idea at the time, but it rarely ends well. That's true for long-term relations, but it's definitely the case on first dates or during the early stages of a relationship. For one thing, consent gets murky after too many drinks. And beyond that, sex is such an intimate and personal act. It's important that both parties are completely present and able to make decisions for themselves.

Forget in vino veritas. Perhaps you've heard the saying "in wine lies the truth" or maybe "a drunk mind speaks a sober heart." Do not buy into this old adage. Many people make the mistake of thinking alcohol will help them address issues in their relationship because of its ability to reduce inhibitions. The problem is, when we're under the influence, we tend to talk more in absolutes and make accusations. Instead of saying, "Would you mind doing this or that differently?" you might say, "You never do this!" or "I hate when you always do that!" Save the serious talks for sober moments when you won't be thinking in black and white.

Take the edge off. There are other ways to deal with anxiety around dating. A friend once gave this advice: anytime you're going on a first date, you should pleasure yourself beforehand so you're not going into the date super horny. It puts you at ease so you can relax and have a good time without your hormones getting in the way. Just saying!

chapter eleven

FAIRY TALE REWRITTEN

Lauren

Like most other girls, I was taught from an early age about the whole Prince Charming fantasy, the perfect man who sweeps you off your feet and leads you to a life of comfort, happiness, and security. My parents didn't push the idea on me, but it was everywhere else. Growing up in the nineties, I saw that television and movies were filled with dashing Mr. Rights—think Carrie Bradshaw's Mr. Big in *Sex and the City*, one of my all-time faves.

The stereotype goes beyond fiction too. I had family that lived in an affluent Detroit suburb. Anytime we visited I was intrigued by the other families in the neighborhood, with the handsome CEO husbands and the stay-at-home wives who seemed to spend their days baking cookies or getting their hair done.

Out of these many impressions, the picture of the perfect man began to take shape in my mind. He was fit from regular workouts with a great job that allotted him time to take care of our family.

He was dressed to kill, so we would always complement each other when we were out on the town. Basically, a lot of superficial qualities were at the forefront of my list. And—surprise, surprise—it didn't result in many healthy relationships.

I wound up dating guys who seemed perfect on paper and checked all the above boxes. They made great money, they had the big house and fancy car, and they radiated charisma. But then they ended up being a cheater or an asshole, or often both. I remember this guy I dated for a while; he was doing very well for himself, really crushing it in his career. We got along well at first, but then he started to become controlling and passive-aggressive. For example, if I put on an outfit I felt sexy in, he'd make some obnoxious remark like, "Oh, you must really be feeling yourself, huh? Who are you trying to look good for?" It made me really think twice about things that *I* loved and felt good about.

This pattern repeated over and over throughout my twenties. At a certain point, I had to admit to myself that MY fantasy of Prince Charming was really more of a nightmare.

Cameron

Like Lauren, I started developing my ideas of romance and relationships at an early age. When I was a kid, my favorite toy was my G.I. Joe action figure. One Christmas, I asked my parents for a Barbie doll. They were kind of freaked out, like, "What's going on here? Why does he want a Barbie all of a sudden?" My grandma wound up getting me a Barbie and my parents were relieved to discover that I only wanted it so that G.I. Joe could have a wife.

I had a fairly traditional view of love and marriage growing up, based largely on the example set by my parents. They had their disagreements over the years, but they always worked through them and were always clearly on the same team. It was the type of relationship I knew I wanted. But the older I got, the more I came to believe that my parents' relationship was the exception and there was a very slim chance that I would ever achieve something similar.

By my twenties, my faith in finding a wife was shaken, because all my serious relationships seemed to end badly. It always felt like I had to be on alert for something to go wrong. I started succumbing to the notion that messy, dysfunctional relationships can be romantic in their own way. I bought into the relationship patterns portrayed in Hollywood: big blowup fights followed by grand, romantic gestures to make up for them. I convinced myself that fighting is a normal part of relationships and held on tight to the idea that every relationship requires work. What I did not want to accept is the fact that some relationships are not meant to be and no amount of work can save them.

My last major relationship before *Love Is Blind* exemplified this kind of relationship. There were a lot of ugly fights and arguments. We'd let unaddressed issues fester until they erupted in a fight, split up for a couple months, then get back together, and the pattern would repeat. I became addicted to the rush of getting back together after periods of hurt and uncertainty. But the lows started to come more frequently, and they kept getting lower and lower. It was not sustainable. It took me longer than I care to admit, nearly five years in fact, to recognize that. Once I did, however, I realized I deserved a healthy relationship and started focusing on the qualities that I did want in a partner in order to be compatible.

Lauren

Part of the destiny of Cam and me is that we both reached this moment of maturity in our outlook on relationships at the same time. We'd taken our licks and were ready to stop wasting our time. I made the decision that I was going to base my feelings for a person on who he is on the inside and not all the superficial stuff that had steered me into bad relationships in the past. I became attracted to conversation instead of wondering about the guy's bank account or how attractive he was. After a date, I'd ask myself questions like: *How does this person make me feel? Does he respect me? Do I feel lighter or heavier after talking with him? Is he taking energy from me or is he adding to me?*

Those questions became the starting point for any potential relationship. The material possessions played second fiddle; if he didn't make me feel good about myself, it was a nonstarter. And a lot of the guys in the pods were nonstarters. The sparks were few and far in between with some of them being intoxicated on our first date, and they didn't leave the best first impression.

And then there was Cam. For starters, I could tell he had a sweet spirit. He was actively listening to the things I shared. Our conversations had depth, at a level that I've only experienced a few times in my life. Then we started to discover all the things we had in common, the shared passions, life goals, and feelings around families. I would come away from dates with Cameron feeling completely light and energized. It was like, *Wow, I've never felt like this before. This is different from your average butterflies. I got whales swimming in my stomach.*

Cameron

I had whales too, and none bigger than on our fifth date. Before filming began, the producers had asked us to bring a gift to the set for the person we formed the deepest connection with. I had the producers deliver two gifts to Lauren on the fifth date. The first was a tote bag that my mom had made. She said she loved the bag, but it was the second gift that really surprised her.

"Oh my God! Is this a plum tree?" Lauren exclaimed through the pod wall.

"Yes, it is. I wanted to give it to you to symbolize the beginning of our relationship and the hope that it will grow over time."

"It's perfect! Thank you."

"You're welcome. My parents also planted two trees in their back-yard when they first got married. That's where I got the idea from."

"That's beautiful. You know, this is extra special because when I was a kid, my dad would take me out on the weekends and whenever we passed by the market, he would buy me plums."

"Wow. It's like the universe is trying to tell us something."

We shared a few moments of silence together. I knew what I was going to say next, though it seemed to happen in slow motion.

"What if I were to propose to you?" I asked.

There was a brief pause; then Lauren responded, "What if I

were to say yes?" The words hit me like a bullet train to the chest. It was like the floor was falling out from under my feet. Just then a voice over the PA announced it was time to wrap up the date.

"Then we would be engaged," I replied.

"I'll talk to you soon, Cameron."

"I'm looking forward to it, Lauren."

"Me too."

What is happening? I thought to myself as I made my way back to the men's lounge. This was supposed to be a fun, two-week adventure and here I was on the verge of proposing. I could feel the torrent of emotions starting to build, so I made a beeline for the gym, with the hope that I wouldn't be bothered there. I needed time to think. I pretended to lift weights in order to avoid suspicion. The producers were on to me, however. As I looked up from the weight rack, while fighting back tears, I saw a camera lens peering around the corner. I put my head back down so they wouldn't see me tearing up. Out of the corner of my eye, I saw a producer talking to Boxer Matt. When I looked up again, he was making his way toward me.

"Hey, buddy, what's going on?" he asked.

"Oh, just lifting weights," I replied with a soft laugh, while still fighting to keep from crying.

"Did you just come back from a date?"

"Yeah. I had a date with Lauren."

"I can tell something happened on that date. What was it?"

"We were talking and then . . . something inside me told me to ask her what would happen if I asked her to marry me."

"And what did she say?"

"She said, 'What if I said yes?'"

"That's amazing, buddy! And how do you feel right now?"

"Overwhelmed, elated . . . scared, knowing that she's the one and that this is going to change everything."

"She's the one?"

"She's the one."

Lauren

The world kind of stopped spinning in that moment for me too. Just five days into the show, my life was changing forever. I couldn't wrap my head around the fact that a little more than a week earlier I'd been in Paris with Tiff, dancing with supermodels and climbing to the top of the Eiffel Tower. Now I was on the verge of getting engaged to this man who seemed to fall out of the sky; he was perfect *for me* in every way.

When Cameron popped the question for real four days later, it was like being in a dream. "You're such a beautiful person," I gushed to him through the wall between us. "I don't have to see you to know that." I would soon get to see everything about his physical attributes at the reveal ceremony, which took place a day later and without question was one of the longest days of my life. We were up filming at 7:00 a.m., but Cam and I were one of the last couples to go (six couples in all made it to the proposal stage). It was probably 9:00 p.m. before they got to us. That meant the majority of the day was spent sitting around contemplating the enormity of the situation. In the pod, we didn't have to think at all about physical appearances. Now I had to think about things like messy hair, sweaty armpits, and bad breath. I was a nervous wreck. But then I reminded myself that's not why I fell in love with Cam. I fell for him because he's sweet, driven, and charismatic. Also because he cares about my happiness in ways that I've never experienced before.

Cameron

The day of the reveal was torture. Myself and the rest of the guys were held in the parking lot outside the facility, and one by one we were called to the reveal ceremony. We all tried to keep our minds occupied by imagining how the ceremony would go: Would there be a big twist? Would we walk into the ceremony only to find out this was all some cruel prank on us? Would we be attracted to our partners? Would anyone change their mind after they met in person? After hours of storytelling, pacing around the parking lot, and staring off into the fields behind the facility, it was finally my turn. By the time the producers came for me, night had already fallen.

As the producer brought me to the room leading to the reveal hallway, he told me to pick a ring when I got inside. Sure enough, as I entered the room and looked around I noticed a small table with a dozen rings glimmering under the studio lights.

I knew I only had minutes to decide. A little voice in my head whispered, *Pick the one with the biggest rock!* Moments later, I spotted the ring that most spoke to me. I picked up the ring, but before I had a chance to truly admire it, Nick Lachey was standing next to me.

"Hey, Cam, are you ready for this?" Nick asked in a serious but excited tone. "This is the biggest moment of your entire life! This is going to change the trajectory of everything that happens to you from now on. Are you ready for that? Are you ready?"

"I'm ready," I answered, decidedly, while doing my best to keep my nervousness in check. At that moment, I couldn't concentrate on anything except what was about to happen. Once Nick wished me luck and left the room, I approached the opaque plexiglass door, through which I could just make out a hallway with a similarly frosted door at the opposite end. I started rocking back and forth on the balls of my feet and taking deep breaths. I tried focusing on slowing down my heartbeat, which felt like it might bruise my chest. I am not sure why exactly, but I was able to calm myself a bit by chanting Lauren's name beneath my breath to steady my nerves: "Lauren Michelle Speed, Lauren Michelle Speed, Lauren Michelle Speed."

All of a sudden, the silhouette of a woman appeared behind the other door. *That couldn't be her, could it?* My skepticism started to spike again. I thought maybe this was a trick and they were going to send a supermodel out to tell me that my fiancée was waiting for me in the back room. But then the doors opened and I knew in an instant that it was Lauren. I started running toward her but slowed my pace when I noticed she seemed to be squinting back at me (I later learned this was because she didn't have her glasses on). As soon as I reached her, I took her into my arms and, at long last, we kissed. I later learned that there were more than two hundred people on set watching the scene unfold, but it felt like just the two of us. I dropped to one knee, pulled out the ring, and popped the question. After she said yes, we embraced again. "I'm going to take care of you," I told her. And that's been my focus ever since.

Lauren

"You literally look like a prince, like Prince Charming," I told Cameron once we finally locked eyes on each other. And isn't it ironic, I spent my whole life looking for Prince Charming, only to end up with one Mr. Wrong after another. Then, as soon as I stopped looking for the fantasy, it fell into my lap in the form of Cameron, my soul mate and life partner. The fact that he's successful, charming, and gorgeous is the icing on the cake. But it's the cake that matters most.

"How did I get so lucky?" I asked, though I knew luck had nothing to do with it. Cameron and I found love because A) it was fate, but B) we were both willing to write our *own* fairy tale.

Thinking Outside the Box

The *LIB* experiment made it easier to focus on the meaningful aspects of our relationship. But even in real life, there are ways to avoid the fantasy pitfalls and find a partner who is truly right for you. Here are a few rules to keep in mind:

Forget about types. Blond versus brunette. Jock versus nerd. We grow up bombarded by stereotypes and it's easy to become romantically attached to certain ones. The problem is, they're very one-dimensional when in reality, people and relationships are incredibly complex. Going on dates with people who aren't your usual type is a great way to get outside your comfort zone and discover new emotional depths.

Trust your instincts. If you have a conversation with someone and you feel drained afterward or even a nervous pit in your stomach, that's the universe telling you that there is a problem that needs to be addressed. It is likely because you have some serious reservation about the person that has yet to be discussed or you have already identified a major incompatibility, whether you acknowledge it consciously or not. At the same time, don't sabotage your happiness by looking for society's fairy tale. If you have that nervous feeling like something could be problematic about the relationship, fight the urge to ignore it and instead express how you are feeling to your partner. At worst, the conversation leads to the end of the relationship, which is still a net gain because it means you have ruled out someone who wasn't right for you. At best, you have a meaningful discussion with your partner that resolves your reservation and deepens your connection.

Don't fall for the idea that love conquers all. Love alone is not sufficient for a healthy relationship, and it is very possible for two people to love each other and still not be right for each other. There has to be a foundation of trust, respect, and compassion in the relationship. There also has to be a willingness to compromise on some things, an unwillingness to compromise on others, and the insight to distinguish between the two. You and your partner both have to have an incredible amount of patience and come to understand that there will be good days and bad, but at the end of each day you both agree that the value you bring to each other's lives outweighs the difficulties. But love alone is not enough. If you want the best for both you and your partner, make sure you have everything else in the relationship as well.

chapter twelve

KISS AND DON'T TELL

Cameron

"Maybe you guys want to try shooting this scene without your robes on," the producer pressed.

It had been less than forty-eight hours since I laid eyes on Lauren for the first time. Immediately following the reveal ceremony on *Love Is Blind*, the crew took us to separate hotels where we were sequestered for a day. I'm not exactly sure why we were separated like that. Maybe they had not expected eight couples (yes, eight!) to get engaged on the show. What I did know is that I was going crazy being alone in my hotel room without a phone or any way to talk to my fiancée!

I was allowed my phone to give my employer a brief call to let him know I would be taking another week off as I had let him know was a possibility. I had told him I was going on a reality show before I left, but hadn't filled in any of the details.

"Did you win?" he asked.

"Yes, I did," I replied, while thinking of Lauren.

"Excellent, excellent . . . I can tell you're really happy, so no worries, Cameron. We will see you in a week."

Production also let me give Mom a call.

"I was starting to get worried when I didn't hear from you," she said.

"Well, I did say that I wouldn't be able to access my phone for the last two weeks."

"Yes, but I was still worried that the show might not be real. I was about ready to come looking for you." We both laughed at that.

After this day of seclusion, Lauren and I were reunited once again. Our producer whisked us to the airport where we boarded a flight to Mexico, eventually ending up at the Grand Velas Riviera Maya in Playa Del Carmen. I wanted to pounce on Lauren from the moment I saw her, and she was giving me the eyes too. We couldn't keep our hands off each other in the airport and were causing enough of a scene that our producer walked ten feet away from us because of his embarrassment. The oceanfront suite and the private Jacuzzi only heightened my anticipation. But Lauren and I weren't about to make soft-core porn for Netflix.

"That's okay; we'll keep them on," I said firmly. We had learned early on that you had to stand your ground with the producers. I don't blame them for always wanting to push the limits. That's what reality television is all about. They were just doing their jobs. But Lauren and I knew our line and there was no crossing it.

There was talk that some of the other couples may have gone further on camera. One couple was rumored to have been filmed having sex in the shower. I can neither confirm nor deny that rumor, but I did notice one of the teasers for the show contained a clip that seemed to align with that rumor. So it is possible that some of us were baring more than our hearts for the camera.

The next morning, the producers wanted Lauren and me to spill the tea on what happened during our first night together.

"How did it go last night?" one of them asked probingly as Lauren and I sipped our coffee and juice.

"Good," I answered.

"Did you sleep in the same bed?" the other producer asked, with a little more urgency.

"Yes, of course."

"Did you cuddle?" the first one asked with a sort of singsongy cadence.

"There was some cuddling involved," I said.

"Oh for Christ's sake, did you have sex or what?!?"

"Can we get some more juice in here?" Lauren asked, with a laugh.

Lauren

Cameron and I got very good at the evasion game. But that doesn't mean we never talked about sex. The subject came up during our early dates in the pods, and it's something we continue to talk about comfortably.

We all know sex is a natural part of life. It's part of the bond that forms between two people who are romantically involved. Unfortunately, the topic is taboo in many parts of our society, so people are often too shy to bring it up. I'm not saying it should be the starter topic on the first date. But if you're sexually attracted to someone or are interested in pursuing them it doesn't hurt to let it be known. Otherwise, you could end up in the friend zone, even though that's not what you're there for. (See "Let's Talk about Sex" [page 128] for tips on starting the conversation.)

I'm not sure where my comfort talking about sex comes from. Definitely not from my parents! I've had exactly two conversations with them, both times with my mom. The first was back in college. I was home from break one semester—not my first year of school, this was closer to my last year. She came into my room one morning and said to me:

"Honey, do you have any questions about sex?"

"I think I'm good, Mom!"

The other time was shortly after Cam and I were married. My mom came to the house for a visit. As soon as Cameron left the room, she slyly pulled a bottle of coconut oil from her luggage and handed it to me.

"This is magic in a marriage," she whispered. "That's all I'm going to say." Once again, my response was along the lines of an awkward, sarcastic "Yea, thanks, Mom!"

Cameron

Well, I appreciated the coconut oil. And I've always told Lauren her mom has good advice. My mom had also tried to talk to me about sex several times during my teenage years. The conversations always followed a similar pattern: Mom would try to broach a topic, like wearing protection, but then we would both be uncomfortable, and she would quickly wrap up the discussion.

124

"You know you can talk to your father or me if you have any questions," she would always say.

"I know, Mom."

While the topic was uncomfortable, I knew it was coming from a good place. And although I can't remember ever asking my parents questions about sex, I think the fact that they always showed that they cared about me and made me feel safe helped me develop a willingness to be vulnerable. I believe to have intimacy of any kind with someone requires an exchange of vulnerability. I realize in retrospect that while parents and children having conversations about sex can be deeply uncomfortable, they can be helpful for the child, who is still trying to figure what to make of it.

Lauren and I don't pretend to have all the answers. Sex is nuanced and different for everyone. Your sex life with your partner continues to evolve as your relationship evolves. But I will share with you what insights have helped us continue to enrich our sex life.

First, sex really needs to be an ongoing conversation with your partner. You should make an effort to check in regularly to see how they are feeling about your sex life. It can be fun and enlightening to talk to your partner about their turn-ons, turnoffs, fantasies, and questions. Ask them what's their favorite thing that you do to them and what they love doing to you. Ask them what they would like more or what they would like less of. Maybe your partner is not as willing to talk about their sexuality, but when they do, listen. Ultimately, sex is more psychological than physical, so understanding more about why they have the turn-ons and fantasies they do can bring new levels of fulfillment to your relationship. Even just feeling heard and accepted for the uniqueness of their sexuality can make your partner feel more connected to you.

Another critical lesson I learned is that encouraging sex is not solely about turning your partner on but also about eliminating the turnoffs from your environment. One of the biggest turnoffs can be stress. While some people have a higher desire for sex when they're stressed as a means of coping with it, others deprioritize sex when stressed. Sex is not immediate to survival, so it makes sense that sex is no longer the focus when people are in a constant state of stress. Consider ways in which you can take some of the burden off your partner's back—whether it is doing more around the house, going on a walk together, making them laugh, whatever you know helps your partner unwind. It is, of course, not only good for your sex life but also good for the general well-being of your partner and your relationship if you are able to find strategies that work for easing their stress.

Another turnoff can be exhaustion. We often have to make adjustments to fit our sex life into our busy schedule. This might be stating the obvious, but it's crucial to make time for intimacy before you are burned out for the day. People often think of the evening hours as the time for sex. But after putting in a hard day's work, Lauren and I aren't always in the mood. We've learned that morning sex is one way of jumping this hurdle. Sometimes exhaustion is difficult to avoid, but by recognizing the importance of sex in your relationship and your well-being, you are better able to prioritize it. Set aside time devoted to dates and other romantic time that you both agree is sacred and will not be disrupted by work.

It also helps to create the mood. Lauren loves flowers, so I might surprise her with roses, light some candles, and throw on a little Sade. I might make reservations at a restaurant with a romantic ambiance or explore a new part of the city with her we've never spent much time in before. It is important to keep having new experiences with your partner: the memories from those experiences often stay with you most strongly. Also, it can't hurt to cook one of your partner's favorite meals.

Lauren

When I come home and Cameron is in the kitchen making his chicken fettuccine Alfredo, I know he's out to seduce me. It usually works, unless we eat too much and slip into a food coma. But, it is important to zhuzh it up every now and then. Now, putting in a little extra effort or paying attention to detail is not a guaranteed ticket to "pum pum town." But small gestures of affection can help lead the way to larger ones.

At the end of the day, the thing to remember is that good sex starts in the mind. Yes, there's the physical act of intercourse between two people. But with *good* sex, a deeper connection occurs, and that's what unlocks the passion. It's the most powerful and positive life force in the world. There are many layers to the love Cameron and I share. But I know I speak for the both of us when I say that passion is one of our favorites. And for any *LIB* producers reading this, we definitely did Netflix and chill that first night in Mexico.

Our "Let's Get It On" Playlist

Here's a list of our favorite mood-making songs:

- ♫ "He Loves Me" —Jill Scott
- ♫ "Kiss of Life" —Sade
- ♫ "The Light" —Common
- ♫ "Comfortable" —H.E.R.
- ♫ "Any Time, Any Place" —Janet Jackson
- ♫ "Good Company" —KYE

Let's Talk about Sex

Sex can be difficult to talk about. But here's the hard truth: if you can't talk openly about sex with your partner, it's going to be more difficult to sustain a healthy sex life with them. The appropriate time to talk about sex can vary from person to person and date to date. Therefore, it may be wise to ease into sexual conversations. As with all things relationship-related, having questions in mind can help get the conversation started and keep it flowing in a positive direction. Here are some things we've asked each other over the years, going all the way back to the pods:

How comfortable are you talking about sex? Start the conversation out slowly. You can see how they respond when talking about sex in a broader sense (e.g., when discussing a movie with a steamy sex scene). If the conversation becomes more personal, be curious and ask questions. Do not try to push the discussion if your partner is indicating they are not interested in continuing the conversation. This applies to couples who have been together for a while as well: open dialogue can make you feel vulnerable, but it will ultimately lead to a more satisfying partnership.

What are your biggest turnoffs? Once you've broken the ice, you can dig a little deeper into your partner's sexuality. Talking about turnoffs, or even embarrassing sexual experiences, is less direct than asking about turn-ons. People tend to have an easier time relating to conflict. If the conversation flows easily, you can move into turn-ons next. Keep the conversation going about what you both like and dislike as the relationship matures, even if you feel like you already understand your partner's sexuality. When discussing turnoffs, pay close attention to not just what they don't like during sex itself but what situational factors reduce their desire for sex, such as stress, routine, and exhaustion. We all have our own unique sexuality that evolves over time, even if those changes are small (e.g., learning that a particular type of outfit your partner wears turns you on, coming up with a new fantasy scenario).

Do you like massages? Massage can do wonders for your sex life because it accomplishes several things at once: 1) it helps relieve your partner's stress, 2) it can stoke the fire of passion by allowing you to take time to appreciate each other's bodies before jumping into the main event, and 3) it is satisfying to give and receive a massage, even if it doesn't always lead to sex. Let your partner know you don't have any expectations for sex and don't get upset if sex doesn't always happen after. Appreciate this sensual exchange not as a means to an end but an end in itself.

What is something you have always wanted to try? Sex is at least as much psychological as it is physical. When you are able to fulfill your partner's fantasies, they will be truly grateful to you. Of course, it is important to let each other know what you are not comfortable with up front to avoid hurt feelings later in the discussion. Once you both have established what you are not comfortable with, start exploring where your partner's mind goes when they fantasize and see where you are willing to meet them. Our fantasies often include dramatic settings, like the penthouse suite of a skyscraper hotel, with big, sweeping views of the city below. Sometimes we may engage in a bit of role play. For example, one of us will play the part of a college professor and the other a student in search of some extra credit. Want to guess who plays which part? Wink wink!

chapter thirteen

MEET THE PARENTS

Cameron

During one of our early pod dates, Lauren and I were talking about family, as we often did. At one point, I heard Lauren say, "Pam and Bill." Those are my parents' names, so I thought I missed something she said or a question she had asked.

"Yeah, my parents' names are Pam and Bill. How did you know that?" I asked.

"What? No, I was saying my parents are named Pam and Bill." There were a few moments of silence as we both tried to process what was happening.

"Wait, your parents are named Pam and Bill?" I asked.

"Yes," Lauren answered, a bit confused at this point.

"My parents are named Pam and Bill!" I shouted.

"Are you messing with me?"

"No, are you messing with me?"

I remember thinking to myself, *Is this some kind of strange mind game that Production is playing on me? Is Lauren in on this?* However, that thought dissipated when I turned my focus back to Lauren and considered how genuine our connection felt. It all felt too good to be true, but I resisted the urge to self-sabotage. I reasoned that while it was possible that this was an elaborate ruse, the love I had already fostered for Lauren was very real and worth taking a leap of faith.

Fun revelations like our parents having the same names and wedding anniversaries one day apart (December 17 and 18) underscored how fated my and Lauren's connection felt. The more we talked about our parents, including the way they raised us, the more we realized how similar our values are. First and foremost, our parents instilled in us the importance of family and of honoring thy mother and father. Our parents also drilled into us the value of hard work from an early age. Lauren and I exchanged stories about how we were both disciplined as children, how our parents had been there for us in times of need, and how they had encouraged us to be well rounded by getting involved in clubs and programs in school. The more we talked, the more I felt like I already knew her parents. I was excited to meet them, even if I'd only known their daughter for a few weeks.

Lauren

Cam might not have had much trepidation about meeting my parents, but I sure did! Not so much with my mom, but with my dad? Definitely. You get to see some of this in the show. With so much of our story line, the tension seemed to be entirely about race—as if my dad was put off by Cameron's race. Although our different backgrounds were addressed by my father it was never his main concern. He just wants to make sure his daughter is with a respectable, intelligent man. My dad and I have always had a close relationship; I wear my "Daddy's girl" title proudly. Growing up, I wasn't going to bring just any guy home to meet my dad. And the truth is that, prior to Cam, I had never introduced any of my boyfriends to my father, because I felt that none of them were worthy enough of the introduction. The fact that I was willing to go there was the biggest indication in my mind of how serious my feelings for Cam were.

I was very anxious about the meeting, so I started prepping Cam days in advance, during our proposal-moon at the resort in Mexico.

"Just to let you know, my dad does not take any shit," I said one morning, apropos of nothing. We were sitting poolside, enjoying a late breakfast. I think it caught Cam a little off guard.

"Okay," he said slowly.

It wasn't that I was afraid Cameron was going to say anything crazy to my dad. Cam is obviously a very thoughtful person and not one to fly off the handle or behave unpredictably. Still, I felt like it was only fair to give him some sort of warning.

"I'm just saying, he speaks his mind," I explained. "So don't be offended. That's just the way he is. No buffer. He's going to grill you hard. But he's doing it out of love."

"I can't wait to meet him," Cam said. And I could tell he really meant it.

Cameron

Meeting the potential in-laws for the first time is going to be stressful for anyone. If it's not, it probably means you're not as emotionally invested as you need to be for this step in the relationship. I think it's important to keep in mind that all parents are protective of their children and want some kind of reassurance that their child's partner is going to take care of them and bring value to their life. The parents are going to err on the side of skepticism until they feel they have enough reason to believe you are willing and capable of making their child happy. It may not be easy at first to convince your future in-laws you are the one for their child, but if your genuine intentions are to take care of your partner and enhance their life in the ways you can, your in-laws will not have much justified ground for disliking you.

I met Lauren's mom a week after returning from our proposal-moon. We had spent our first week living together in an apartment in Atlanta. It was a difficult week: we were no longer in paradise and had to deal with balancing our normal responsibilities with the fact that our wedding was less than four weeks away. Lauren became withdrawn and I knew a major contributor to that was her concern over how her parents would react to meeting me. I was becoming anxious as well, as it was difficult to see her so reserved after all the romance we shared in Mexico. I wanted to put her mind at ease.

I was ready to meet my soon-to-be mother-in-law when the day finally came. I gave Lauren and her mom a chance to catch up before returning to the apartment from work. When I walked in, I was relieved: she greeted me with a warm smile and a hug.

I could tell Lauren gets her quieter and more gentle side from her mom.

"So . . . why do you want to marry my daughter?" she asked in a soft and cheerful tone.

"Lauren is the most amazing woman I have ever met," I began. "Although we have only known each other for a few weeks, I have been able to be more vulnerable and transparent with her than with anyone else in my life. I love and respect her deeply and I know we can make each other happy."

"Wow, so you're really serious then?" she replied, still smiling.

"I am."

"Well . . . that's good to hear."

We continued getting to know each other until one of the producers appeared and led Momma Speed off to another room.

When she returned, she said, "So, Lauren tells me you like to rap?"

I laughed to myself, knowing where this was going. "Yeah, I like to rap."

"Can you . . . ?"

"You want me to rap right now? Okay."

While I would happily oblige any request from Lauren's mom, I could tell immediately that Production was behind this. I performed the cleanest rap I could think of, but I was cursing Production out in my mind for the image I knew they were trying to paint. Sure enough, when we watched the rap once the show came out, my fears had come true: they edited it to sound as bad as possible! Not only did they superimpose a beat that didn't match my tempo; they also cut segments out and rearranged others, such that it sounded totally off beat and clumsy. One of the producers later posted the unedited rap she had recorded with her phone, and the differences between that one and the version on the show are jarring. I generally accepted the edits of me as accurately representing who I am, with the exception of this rap. But I digress.

Cringe-worthy editing aside, meeting Lauren's mom further assured me everything was unfolding as it was supposed to. As Lauren recapped how she thought the meeting went to the cameras, her mom and I stepped out into the hallway so we could continue chatting. Within the first few minutes, she was asking about our plans for starting a family.

"So, what do you think about having kids?" she asked.

"Well, I know all of this is happening really fast, but after Lauren and I spend a few years together as a married couple we talked about having kids," I replied.

"I'm ready for some grandkids," she said with a smile.

Meeting Lauren's dad was higher stakes, as she had made it clear he would not be as receptive as her mom. I knew how close Lauren and her dad are, and I also knew he was protective based on Lauren's warnings. She seemed to be getting more and more tense as the meeting day approached. She basically told me that her father's response to me would determine how comfortable she felt moving forward with the wedding. The pressure was on, but I tried to keep calm and remind myself that my intentions were good, so I didn't have anything to worry about.

I relied on this reasoning to keep my nerves in check when the meeting day finally arrived. I wasn't worried about impressing him; rather, I was focused on assuring him I truly cared for his daughter and that I was fully committed to her. After Lauren left the room and it was just the two of us, he immediately volleyed a stream of questions. "What kind of life can you give my daughter?" he asked. "Have you ever been in a room full of Black people and been the only white guy in there?" "Do you think you'll be able to keep up with her lifestyle?" "How do I know this isn't just some rushed decision?" "Did you consider asking for my blessing before you proposed to her?"

With each new question, I sensed he was looking to rattle me and was pushing harder to find out what would. However, even in that moment, I understood why he was grilling me the way he was. I put myself in his shoes and asked how I would feel if Lauren were my daughter and she intended marrying some man she met on a reality TV show. I would have grilled the hell out of that guy. With all that in mind, my focus was on putting his mind at ease by conveying the ways I planned to take care of his daughter and expressing what she meant to me. I also emphasized that I did not want to take anything away from her life or change her; I only wanted to add to her life in the ways I could. By the end of the conversation, I knew I had softened his resistance, but had not completely sold him on the idea of our marriage.

I think many people make the mistake of trying to impress their partner's parents with their credentials and accomplishments. Instead, I think the focus should be on your level of commitment. It's also important to show the extent to which you and their child have discussed major life decisions and core values. If Lauren and I hadn't talked through the most critical aspects of our future lives—kids, finances, the dynamics of a mixed-race relationship, sex, conflict resolution, blending families, balancing time together with alone time, even the division of household chores—the cracks would have quickly shown under the pressure of her father's inquisition.

Lauren

Cameron definitely passed the test. "He's almost too cool," my dad said later. "He didn't break a sweat." I think he would've enjoyed seeing Cameron squirm just a little! But I was so relieved to see the relationship between my fiancé and my parents start out on stable ground.

My meeting Cam's parents unfolded differently, in part because they're still married and reside in Maine, so they flew in just for our meeting. This was after the proposal-moon and a couple weeks before the wedding day.

The plan was to meet at Cam's house, then have my parents join us as well. Because we were under the accelerated timeline of the show, it made sense to handle all the meetings at once. That added to the pressure, but I was happy to get it all over at once.

When I reached the house, Cam was there to greet me at the front door. There were some nerves, of course, but like Cam said, we had spent so many hours talking about our families and our future lives together. It was like that feeling in school of going into a test 100 percent prepared. You're still nervous, but you know the material front and back.

Cam led me into the living room and introduced me to his mom and dad. The first impression was very warm and welcoming. His mom and I quickly made our way into the kitchen. Like me and my dad, Cam and his mom are very close, so I made sure to tread lightly at first, following her lead with the conversation. After a few minutes of small talk, I showed her my wedding dress and conversation began to blossom. But we took our time and started the journey of learning about each other. I think the temptation in this situation is to try to become fast friends, but in-law relationships need breathing room. They need to develop over time. Even when the two parties hit it off instantly, it takes time for a true relationship to develop.

That said, I felt like Cam's mom and I had plenty to bond over. We're both nurturers; we like to take care of people, especially our families, almost to an overprotective degree—you know, the mother hen personality type. We're also both creative. I like to eat and she likes to cook, so we're a perfect match in that regard! That first meeting with Cam's mom only confirmed how right my and Cam's union felt, no matter how unorthodox the circumstances.

Cameron

With my past couple serious relationships, my parents were extremely skeptical after meeting the girl for the first time. Like Lauren's dad, my parents have always been protective and have wanted to ensure my partner has my best interests in mind. So it was a huge relief when my mom pulled me aside after she and Lauren chatted in the kitchen. "Well, I had my doubts about this whole thing," my mom said. "But Lauren seems like a good person, very sweet and thoughtful. I can see why you chose her." I almost couldn't believe what I was hearing, since my parents had never endorsed anyone I had dated. The universe was continuing to make way for me and Lauren!

Soon after, Lauren's dad showed up and the five of us sat down together in the living room. Of course, everyone was a little nervous and restrained at first. But I kept reminding myself that this was a normal milestone and I should lean into it.

"Wow, this is crazy, right?" Lauren's dad said finally, breaking the ice. "But it seems like these two kids are really in love with each other."

"Yes, Pam and I were just saying before you arrived how pleasantly surprised we are to see how well they complement each other," Dad replied. "Although this is all happening very fast, it's clear Lauren is a wonderful young lady and that they have found something special in each other."

The conversation eventually turned to race. We all started talking about the prejudice that exists in the world today and what that might mean for our family moving forward. "I just don't want your children to be treated badly because of the color of their skin," Mom said, with her voice trembling as she held back tears. "I don't want them to suffer because of how society treats them and I don't want you two to suffer either." It led to an honest discussion about racism in our society and the challenges it will present to Lauren and me as we continue expanding our family.

"As parents, Lauren and I will be dedicated to giving our children the best lives possible," I said. "We know that there will be times in their lives that people will treat them unfairly, but we will make sure they know they have two parents that love them and teach them to love themselves. You know, I feel that it's ultimately a blessing to have children, even if they have to face certain hardships, even if they're discriminated against. And they will have four grandparents that will also love them and teach them more about where they come from."

This idea that we would all be working together toward the same future struck a very beautiful note, which is funny because none of the meeting made it into the show. Production later said that there were technical issues with the audio. Perhaps that is true. However, I speculate that these sentimental moments of harmony and empathy were often left out because they were not as dramatic as, say, dogs drinking wine or fights about sexual performance. I don't think the producers ever imagined that their *LIB* experiment would lead to the genuine connection between Lauren and me. It was a force bigger than television, and some of the most beautiful moments ended up on the cutting room floor.

Lauren

Of course, *we* can't edit out the memory of those first meetings. And the family dynamic has continued to flourish ever since. It happens one conversation at a time, every small gesture forming another point of connection. It's in the calls to Maine. It's in the visits to my mom's house. It's in the regular Sunday night dinners that we have with my dad. It's been particularly wonderful watching him and Cameron bond, given my initial fears. My dad has expressed how important it is to him that he wants to feel comfortable and confident with passing the torch to the man who will take care of his daughter. It warms my heart to know that he fully supports Cam and I. He actually refers to him as his son. He doesn't like the term "son-in-law." When we're meeting someone new, he always says, "This is my daughter. And this is my son."

Dos and Don'ts When Meeting the In-Laws

Every relationship is different, just like every family is different. There's no playbook for navigating the first meeting of soon-to-be in-laws, but here are some pretty universal tips to keep in mind:

Do focus on your partner. The more you emphasize everything you love about your in-laws' child and how you intend to support them, the more your in-laws will appreciate you. Put yourself in their shoes and consider what reservations they may have so you can address them. In time, they might take more of an interest in you, but in the beginning, they just want to feel confident that you love their child for who they are and will do everything in your power to make them safe and happy.

Do find common ground. This advice applies to finding a partner but also to finding harmony with your partner's parents. In the same way you look for common ground when you first start dating or building a friendship, you want your in-laws to be able to relate to you on some level, whether it's sports, favorite books, TV shows, or a shared hobby. You already share one major thing in common: you both love their child! A good starting ground is to see if your in-laws have any stories they like to tell about your partner. It can also be fun to talk about quirks your partner has and see if there are things your partner's been doing since they were little. It is not enough to simply convince your in-laws to accept your union with their child; you want to foster a relationship with them that will stand the test of time. Your partner will appreciate the bond you have formed with their parents and it will likely strengthen your marriage as well. Plus, family is sacred and the opportunity to expand it is priceless. Of course, no extended family is perfect, and you might not love everyone on your partner's side. But it's important to at least maintain mutual respect. In the words of Jay-Z, "Nobody wins when the family feuds." That's the truth.

Do respect family rules and traditions. Your parents might be cool with you and your partner sharing a room when you come to visit. But if your significant other's parents are more traditional, you need to respect that. Even if your partner is against the policy, show empathy with the in-laws by agreeing to separate rooms.

Don't be fake. You want the meeting to go well and for everyone to get along. Your in-laws will likely be able to tell if you're being genuine or not. It's best to be yourself, while also conveying a desire to bond as a family (and we hope you have that desire). You should offer to help when a family meal is being prepared, for example, but if your help is refused, turn your attention to getting to know the in-laws better through conversation. If you don't know what to talk about, you can always ask them questions about what your significant other was like growing up; parents generally like reminiscing about raising their kids.

Don't get defensive. Right or wrong, parents are naturally inclined to look for potential deal breakers in their child's partner. It is their job to protect their child! During that first meeting and possibly several meetings after, they're going to be looking for things to criticize, even if they trust their child's autonomy and judgment. Try not to take their skepticism or hard line of questioning personally—just take it in stride and work on resolving their resistance while remaining calm.

Keep it casual! Look for a relaxed setting for the first meeting as opposed to a formal dinner or big party setting. Breakfast and brunch are both good options, since everyone's energy will be high, plus you won't have to spend the entire day worrying. Resist the urge to calm your nerves with alcohol so you can have a clear mind going into your meeting. This is your opportunity to communicate your commitment to their child and how you intend to fit into their life moving forward.

chapter fourteen

OUR WHIRLWIND
WEDDING DAY

Lauren

I might have gotten over the whole Prince Charming myth, but I never stopped dreaming about the fairy-tale wedding. Like most women, I was conditioned to believe that this is one of the most important days of your life. So while my idea of what constituted a perfect partner evolved, I still couldn't wait to play the part of princess on my wedding day. I imagined shopping for dresses with my mom. I dreamt about the bridal shower in the weeks leading up to the big day. I got excited thinking about a ratchet bachelorette party, somewhere wild like Las Vegas or Miami.

Instead, I was getting a made-for-reality-TV wedding planned by the production company with their best interest at heart over mine. Don't get me wrong, I knew that I was getting the chance to marry the man of my dreams thanks to this unconventional *LIB* experiment. But I had a hard time getting past the fact that my special day was going to be largely out of my hands. I wanted more time for Cam and me to get to know our respective family and friends. I wanted the two of us to go on cake tastings together and figure out the perfect music. I wanted to go shopping for dresses with my mom and no one else. I'm not going to lie, the whole situation made me distressed. I know it's what I signed up for when I agreed to the show. But I hadn't fully considered how hard it would be to give up the wedding I had been planning in my head from childhood, probably because I didn't really believe I would actually find my husband through this crazy reality TV experiment.

Cameron

For my part, I'd never had any fantasies about my wedding day, so it was much easier for me to accept the unconventional state of affairs. Still, I could tell that not being able to have the wedding she'd always envisioned was taking its toll on Lauren. It was difficult to process at first, because we had just come back from our proposal-moon—the most romantic week of my life—and now Lauren was clearly stressed about our wedding.

On top of Lauren's obvious anxiety about the wedding, her aunt passed away during that period. I came home after work one day to find Lauren wrapped in a blanket, silently crying. She told me what had happened and I asked her what I could do.

"I just need some space to grieve. It's nothing against you, but with all the filming and the wedding and now my aunt passing, I need to be alone."

"Okay. I'll give you some space. I love you."

Christmastime with
the Speed family.
Lauren Speed-Hamilton

The legendary Hamilton Christmas starts young
(our 1997 pictured here). *Pamela Hamilton*

Man's best friend.
Cameron Hamilton

My previous life as a wilderness firefighter. *Cameron Hamilton*

Cuba was nothing short of magical. *Lauren Speed-Hamilton*

Italy was a place I dreamed of visiting my whole life, fueled by my love of pasta and wine. *Lauren Speed-Hamilton*

Behind the scenes of Pod Life! *Love Is Blind* was a life-changing experience.
Michael Hartz

A beautiful little oasis in the forest for a *Love Is Blind* date.
Nieshia Crawford

Our time in Mexico on *Love Is Blind* was so special.
Nieshia Crawford

Moving into our apartment on *Love Is Blind*. Our first home together!
Michael Hartz

So many emotions on our
wedding day, but the main
one is happiness.
Nieshia Crawford

Love and family are our greatest gifts. *Nieshia Crawford*

Our second Thanksgiving together. *Lauren Speed-Hamilton*

Been a Daddy's girl my whole life! My sense of humor, charisma, and business savvy all came from Poppa Speed! *Cameron Hamilton*

Summer lovin' in Atlanta. *Lauren Speed-Hamilton*

My ultimate role models. I'm proud to be a son and brother.
Cameron Hamilton

Art is our inspiration.
Lauren Speed-Hamilton

Dressed up for date night
out to the theater!
Cameron Hamilton

Sparx! Named after the sparks that flew when we met.
Cameron Hamilton

My fur baby. *Cameron Hamilton*

Love Is Blind premiere party.
It's happening!
Lauren Speed-Hamilton

On the go in New York! A whirlwind
of new experiences on the press tour.
Lauren Speed-Hamilton

Capping off an incredible week talking about *Love Is Blind*! If you look closely, you can see the Hollywood sign in the back.
Lauren Speed-Hamilton

Squeezing in a Knicks game during our press tour.
Lauren Speed-Hamilton

Backstage at the reunion episode with our friend Diamond.

Cameron Hamilton

Magical date night guaranteed at the Atlanta Botanical Garden.

Cameron Hamilton

Quarantine meant months at home, but we still made it special
by cooking dinner together—our favorite low-key date night!
Lauren Speed-Hamilton

A Jeep surprise! A symbol of independence and adventure for Lauren.
Cameron Hamilton

We started our YouTube channel "Hanging with the Hamiltons" to share more about our lives and tell the stories we want to tell. Some of our best videos are the ones where we make each other laugh. *Lauren Speed-Hamilton*

Hamilween.
Welcome to the greatest
show on earth!
Demetrious Williams

Celebrating our second anniversary in style! *Robot Booth*

Always and forever. *LaJoy Photography*

"I love you too."

It was difficult to give her space when I saw how distraught she was. My natural tendency is to want to "fix" things by talking through them. But I learned that it is better to respect your partner's wishes when they are going through something, rather than trying to impose your own approaches on them. I began to understand that the more I give her the alone time she needs, the stronger our connection is when we do spend time together.

The day after her aunt passed, we had to go to the courthouse to apply for our marriage certificate. Lauren's hands were shaking so much while filling it out, we had to start over a couple times. We sat down on the steps outside the courthouse after finally submitting the application.

"What do you want to do?" I asked her.

"I know I love you, Cameron," she said. "And I know I want to marry you. I just don't know if I want to marry you one week from now. I just wish we had more time."

It was hard to hear that she was still unsure about getting married, but at the same time I understood. If we really loved each other and wanted to get married, what was the rush? It was the format of the show that was pushing this accelerated timeline, all in the name of entertainment. Of course, we wanted to blame Production for how unfair it seemed to have to abide by this timeline, but the truth was we knew what the deal was going into this experiment. But this was the rest of our lives! It was easy to agree to the conditions of the experiment when I thought there was little chance I would be engaged. Now that I had found the love of my life and she was uncertain about getting married in a couple weeks, I had learned the hard way not to try and predict the future. At this point, I did not know what to expect. All I knew for sure was I wanted to be with Lauren, married or not.

All that in mind, I was still resolute that I was ready to marry Lauren. Her reservations led me to further evaluate if there was anything I was missing, any reason we should not get married in a couple weeks' time. I ran through all the counterfactuals I could think of: What if one of us has to take a job opportunity somewhere else? What if we suffered a loss together? What if we started to get bored in our marriage later on? Would we be able to work through a vast disagreement in the future if neither one of us was willing to compromise? The list goes on. What I confirmed for myself was that there was no one else I would rather face any challenge with than Lauren. Sure, I realized there are always more people out there to date. But I had done my fair share of dating and no one had ever made me feel remotely as sure about our relationship as Lauren. She was and is the one. I didn't need any more time to figure that out.

Once I put to rest that last bit of uncertainty, I felt a sense of calm about where I stood. Still, I wanted to know what Lauren would say on our wedding day, but she was transparent about the fact that she was still deciding. I resisted the urge to try to convince her that it was the right decision. Instead, I did my best to be as supportive as possible, to see things from her perspective, and to put my own selfishness aside.

Lauren

Cameron's kindness helped me sort through the uncertainty, but I was still tied up in knots over the prospect of tying the knot. Even the logistics of the invite list left me paralyzed by indecision. Cameron was excitedly getting his list together, but all I could think about was having to explain this insane story dozens of times over. I kept playing the conversation in my mind:

Me: Hey there, I'm calling to invite you to my wedding.
Them: Wedding? I didn't even know you were dating.
Me: Yeah, well, that's the thing. I went on a reality dating show and met my future husband.
Them: Oh!
Me: And the wedding is in two weeks.
Them: Oh!!!

The deeper I spiraled into these imaginary conversations, the more absurd the whole situation seemed. One morning I called up my mom in tears.

"You know, even if you weren't on this crazy reality show," she said, "and the wedding wasn't happening under such unusual terms, you would probably be having a lot of the same feelings." That provided some comfort, hearing that most brides go through some version of this freak-out. But I still felt like I needed some serious "me time" to make sense of the situation. About a week before the wedding, I approached Cameron with that request.

"The next time we have a day off from filming, I want to be alone," I told him. "I'm going to spend a night or two at my apartment. I just need some time to myself to mentally breathe." I knew this was going to make Cameron anxious, but if there was any chance of my making it down the aisle, it was something I had to do. Cam is right that times of crisis call for empathy from your partner, but it's also important to make sure you're giving yourself the necessary self-care. As long as there's good communication, those two needs can be met simultaneously.

That time alone in my apartment was so important to the process. I basically sat on the couch and alternated between writing in my journal and praying. At a certain point, I opened a bottle of wine, turned up the music, and danced alone in the living room. I reflected on my *Eat, Pray, Love* phase from a year earlier, the trips to Cuba, Italy, and France, and all the soul-searching that I'd done in that time.

I took in my apartment, the artwork that I'd carefully selected and the many little keepsakes and curios that made the space my own. I thought to myself, *Wow, I'm about to leave this all behind.* But instead of filling me with fear, the thought brought comfort. In that moment, I realized that I wasn't leaving this life behind. I was using it as the foundation for a new life with Cameron. The travels, the apartment, the self-reflection, all that work is what made it possible for me to do *Love Is Blind,* find Cameron, and fall in love.

I danced to one more song in the living room—"Kiss of Life" by Sade—then sat back down on the sofa. I was still a jumble of nerves over the wedding planning, but there was finally a stillness in my heart. I picked up the phone and tapped on Cameron's name.

"Hey, babe," he answered.

"Hi, Cameron," I said. We talked for a couple minutes. I could feel his nervous tension through the line.

"So I've made a decision," I said finally.

"Okay, what did you decide?" he asked.

"I've decided that I'm going to say '*I do.*'"

There was an audible gasp on the other end of the phone.

"That's wonderful," Cam said. We both started to laugh, and the laughter soon turned to tears of relief, joy, and ecstasy. I was over the moon.

Cameron

That was a moment too incredible for words. Through this extraordinary journey, that one little phone call left me feeling like I had ascended to heaven. I'd been on edge for the last few days, jittery and unable to concentrate. But in a moment, those feelings were washed away and replaced with the solace of knowing that everything was going to be okay.

That's a good thing too, because the final days of wedding preparations were a whirlwind. Of course, a big part of the premise of *Love Is Blind* is getting hitched on an accelerated timeline. As I mentioned, we mostly knew what we signed up for. Still, there were parts of the process we never could have predicted.

One morning we got a call from a producer. "Hey, we need you guys to pick out your rings in the next hour," he said. After receiving a link to a ring website from the crew, we quickly reviewed the options together, settling on a simple yet elegant pair.

So many decisions were made on the fly. Each day was another hallmark of the wedding-planning process. One day we had the cake testing and our dance rehearsal in the same morning. As Lauren already said, it was a logistical headache determining the guest list based on who might be able to attend on such short notice. We both limited our guest list to our closest family and friends whom we felt we needed there the most. While most of my family and friends were shocked to hear the story of Lauren's and my adventure, I was amazed at how many of them dropped what they were doing and flew down to support me.

The week leading up to the wedding, Lauren and I stayed at our respective places. We figured it would give us an opportunity to mentally prepare for what was about to come and, after the most intense six weeks of our lives, we needed some time to reflect. That said, we did stop by each other's place a couple times for a visit.

The night before the wedding, my twenty or so guests gathered at my house to celebrate. Friends were taking turns recounting some of the wilder things I had done that they had witnessed, but all agreed this took the cake. It was a blessing to spend that time with friends and family from all stages of my life and to have them all together in my home.

The next morning, we made our way to the wedding venue, a historic mansion in Buckhead called The Estate. The scene was organized chaos; a thousand moving parts and everyone moving a hundred miles an hour in all different directions. Eventually, the producers led me and the rest of the groom's party into the waiting room, which turned out to be the wine cellar. It was freezing down there. There was also a strange, nervous energy in the room. After filming day and night for seven weeks, I had started to take being in front of a camera for granted. I didn't take stock of how weird and abnormal it must have been for my loved ones to see me getting married on television while surrounded by cameras themselves. Also, even though I didn't grow up dreaming about my wedding day, I did always think this particular moment would be more celebratory, with lots of laughs, cheers, and champagne popping. Instead, everyone had deer-in-the-headlights, or should I say deer-in-the-spotlight, looks.

I tried talking to my groomsmen and sister (my best person), but everyone was rather reserved. I could see in their faces they were overwhelmed by being thrown into a new reality that I had come to accept over the last two months. I made my way over to Mom, who is never at a loss for words. She told me that she was having trouble accepting this big step in my life, as she still saw me as her little boy. But Mom also expressed that she trusted my judgment and thought Lauren was a wonderful woman from the short time she had spent with her. She asked me if I was worried Lauren was going to say "I don't."

"I just don't want you to get your heart broken," she said.

"I am taking a leap of faith."

"Even in the most sure situations, it's still a leap of faith."

It was difficult to see how hard this change was for her. Yet her final words were the reassurance I needed to make my way to the altar.

After what felt like an eternity, it was time to walk down the aisle. The crew ushered my mom and me to the ceremony room. I hadn't felt a rush like this since waiting behind the plexiglass doors to see Lauren for the first time. Back then, I was about to see her as my fiancée. This time, I would be seeing her as my bride.

"Well, this is it, Cameron," my mom said. "Are you ready?"

"I'm ready," I said.

The door opened onto a surreal scene, with flowers, crystal chandeliers, and a harpist plucking a beautiful and ethereal melody. I would have been happy with plastic flowers and a cake from the grocery store. But I was impressed with the décor and ambiance.

Purely by chance, most of my guests were dressed in blue and red, while Lauren's side was in purple and red. So even the colors seemed to coordinate. I took my mom's arm and we made our way down the aisle.

Lauren

"Surreal" is definitely the word. Standing on the other side of that door with my father, I remember thinking, *Is this really happening? Is this just one long dream? Am I just going to wake up?* The day had been good, nevertheless full of emotion. At one point, the producers had sat me down to talk with my mom. I don't know if they put her up to this, but she said, "So here we are, giving you away to start your OWN family." That triggered me and I started bawling.

"Mom, how could you say that?" I cried. Throughout the entire process, it had been so important for me to maintain my identity. I didn't want to lose myself and I didn't want to feel like I was losing my family. So my mom's words hit deep.

"Oh, I didn't mean it like that," she said, walking back the comment. "I'm proud of you and I know that you guys will be great."

"Mom!" I shouted. "You know you can't play around with my nerves like that." I pretended to be more upset than I was, which I liked to do with my mom, since she would always respond by being extra comforting. It was one of those mother/daughter routines that we'd done since I was young. And in that moment, I needed *a lot* of extra TLC!

"I'm sorry, baby, I'm sorry!" my mom cried, and gave me a big old hug. "You know I'll always be here and I'll always be your mom." We hugged and I started to feel better, more grounded.

As I was standing outside the ceremony room with my dad, seconds away from walking down the aisle, the nerves were firing again. The doors opened and I could see our families sitting there. I saw my mom, smiling through tears. I saw the harpist and thought to myself, *Ooh, this is fancy.* Then I saw Cameron, and he immediately started crying. At that, my dad started crying as well and soon everybody in the place was in tears. My instinct in those moments is to use humor to lighten the mood, so that's what I did as we made our way to the altar, hamming it up with friends and relatives. But before long I was crying too.

Honestly, the rest of the ceremony was a blur. Obviously, I've since watched clips of it on the show, but in my mind's eye it's just a patchwork of beautiful flashbacks—looking over at my family, seeing my brother make his now famous confused facial expressions, staring into Cameron's eyes. And I remember the pastor saying, "I now pronounce you man and wife." Cameron and I kissed before turning around and walking back down the aisle past a sea of smiling faces.

Once we made it through the doors, we had a quick moment to ourselves.

"We really did it," Cameron said.

"We're really married," I said.

And that was that. Then we sang and danced the night away.

Cameron

Well, we wanted to dance the night away. The fact of the matter was, this was still a reality show wedding and there were still more shots to film. We barely had a chance to take in what part of the reception we were at before we were shuffled on to the next event: "Now it's time for your first dance! . . . Now it's time to cut the cake! . . . Now it's time for speeches!" We did not get the chance to savor the traditional reception moments. While it was frustrating to be rushed through our reception, I was on cloud nine after Lauren said "I do"; nothing phased me that night. I understood that the crew was tired from having worked incredibly hard over those seven weeks, and I greatly appreciated everything they did to make the experience a success. Still, I could sense that our guests were tired with all the rushing around. Even Lauren's dad, with his background in production, was a little bothered.

Lauren

A little bothered? Oh no, he was pissed off! In the middle of the reception, once Production had gotten enough tape, they made Cameron take his tux off so that they could return it. Not the classiest choice. And yeah, my dad went off on everybody. "You couldn't wait until the end of the wedding?!" I heard him shout.

But you know what, everyone still had fun. There was an open bar, at least, so everyone had plenty of drinks. It was great to see everyone on the dance floor, including the two Pams and the two Bills. And Cameron in his T-shirt!

Cameron

There was a total sense of euphoria on the dance floor. I don't even remember when the cameras stopped rolling. All I remember was the elation I felt that Lauren and I were married and we had the rest of our lives to continue our journey. I can remember Lauren's aunt coming over and blowing bubbles on us. It was almost an out-of-body experience, one that made my frustrations with Production fade away. And while I was frustrated with Production at various points throughout the journey, as I have noted in this book, when I looked at my bride and all my loved ones around me I felt a profound appreciation for Production's role in bringing this all together. While Lauren's and my relationship and love for each other is completely our own, they provided an environment that helped foster our relationship. Out on the dance floor, with the music blaring and the bubbles floating overhead, it was like Lauren and I were the only two people on earth. I might not have been dreaming about my wedding day my entire life, but I realized that this was the wedding I always wanted.

How to Savor Your Wedding Day

Our made-for-TV wedding was hardly typical, but we still came away with a few insights into what it takes to make the most of the occasion:

Focus on empathy. It's easy to get caught up in one's own needs and desires. There is also a lot of noise around a wedding, with friends and family chiming in and the constant barrage of questions from various vendors. It's vital to focus your attention back on your partner and talk to them about whether they have any reservations about the wedding and what you can do to alleviate their concerns. If you have a difference in opinion about details of the wedding planning, try putting yourself in their shoes to understand where they're coming from. Daily check-ins are always good in a relationship, but they are especially important in the weeks leading up to your wedding day.

Stay on the same page. This is achieved through constant communication. In theory, there should not be any surprises when you get to the altar. Long beforehand, you have to let your partner know your reservations or things that are bothering you about the relationship, even at the risk of hurting their feelings. Open, honest dialogue—like the phone call we had when Lauren confirmed her intention to say "I do"—is the best way to avoid any kind of pitfall on the wedding day and throughout your marriage.

Stay centered and present. You can never get the day back, so you want to be as present as possible. Everyone is different, but for many people, it's good to start the mental preparations a few days before the wedding. That might mean taking an entire day to yourself at some point. Or maybe you need to surround yourself with a few friends who are best at helping you center yourself. A wedding is such a whirlwind experience; you want to enter into it in a state of stillness and calm. Then, once the madness begins, do what it takes to stay present, even if that means disappearing to the bathroom for a few minutes to collect your thoughts and emotions.

Enlist the help of others. Pull together your support group for the big day. This might include the BFF you can count on to rescue you from conversations with any crazy guests. Or the sibling or cousin who is sure to get the dance floor going. It's hard to juggle having fun while staying composed during your wedding. With your support system in place, you'll have fewer things to think about, which will make it easier to focus on enjoying your day.

Part III

chapter fifteen

HONEYMOON IN THE DARK

Cameron

Over the course of dating in the pods, becoming engaged, and getting married, the cameras were rolling sixteen out of twenty-four hours most days for seven weeks straight. It had become normal to have someone reaching down my shirt to attach a microphone or for me to talk about starting a family with Lauren while surrounded by cameras and producers. But as quickly as we had been transported to the world of *Love Is Blind* on the sound stage of Pinewood Atlanta Studios, we were pulled back into our quiet lives. We didn't hear much about the show for six months, despite several attempts to contact Production. We wanted to know what would happen next, but instead Lauren and I spent many nights lying in bed unpacking what we called the "trauma of *LIB*." While the show enabled us to find each other and experience some of the happiest times of our lives, the intensity of it all was overwhelming to reflect on. I spent many hours analyzing everything I said and did while being constantly filmed. *How would they edit me? What dates in the pod would they show? What happened with the other couples? How would they portray Lauren's and my relationship?* I reassured myself that everything would be fine because I was proud of how I handled myself, but the specter of other reality dating shows still loomed in my mind.

During the filming of the show, we would often complain to each other, "Why can't all these cameras just go away?!" We were really looking forward to that time alone and the opportunity to build our relationship with just the two of us. But there was an initial period of withdrawal when it felt like something was missing. We even experienced ghost microphone syndrome: I'd reach down to my shirt, thinking there was a microphone clipped there, but the only ones listening were Lauren and I. Sometimes we would check the cupboards for a hidden camera or expect to see a crew van pulling into the driveway. The unconventional way we fell in love and fostered our relationship had become normal for us, and adjusting to the quiet, private life we had been craving was a challenge, at least at first.

Lauren

Yes, that was intense. Like Cameron said, it had been go, go, go for seven straight weeks. Then after the wedding, everything disappeared. We had recently made the move into Cam's house, and were transitioning into our new lives. I remember waking up earlier than usual one morning. I went downstairs, sat at the kitchen counter, and thought to myself, *Wow, I'm really married! With a whole husband!* Sure, I'd been a girlfriend before. But this was different. In that initial period of transition, I struggled to find my rhythm. After all, so much had changed so rapidly in such a short amount of time. I was trying to find my footing and figure out how my and Cameron's lives fit together. I contemplated seeing a therapist but decided to work it out on my own, with support from Cam, and by throwing myself back into my work. (Let me note: Throughout the entire *LIB* experience, there was no therapist. So all of us worked through these deep emotional caverns on our own. Looking back, I think we all could have benefited from a resident therapist.)

Cameron

I think a post-wedding therapy session is probably a good idea for anyone, as couples go through a period of time where they're transitioning into the psychology of being married. In our case, those feelings were complicated by our sudden cohabitation. In the typical arc of a relationship (at least in the US), a couple dates for six months to a couple years, then they move in together. After they feel comfortable living together, they get married. Our relationship did not fit that mold: we had not experienced years of going on dates, having and resolving disagreements, and learning how to live with each other—we experienced weeks of it. It was especially hard for Lauren to adapt to living together. For one thing, she *really* loved her apartment back in Buckhead, and she continued to hang on to it. She was also hesitant to come into my house and start changing everything around.

A week or so after the wedding, we were at home unpacking her things, including a box with some of her favorite books. I could tell she wasn't sure what to do with them. I went over to the bookcase and cleared one of the shelves.

"Here you go; you can put them here," I said.

"Oh no, Cameron, you don't have to—" she started.

"It's okay," I interrupted. "We're married. This is our home now. This bookcase is as much yours as it is mine." She looked deep into my eyes but didn't say anything. After a few moments of silence, I told her, "It's going to take time for both of us to adjust to sharing our lives, but I know we'll get there."

She replied with a soft, "Yup."

Like many couples, Lauren and I wanted this transition to happen right away. But that's not how it works. I'll admit, I would get nervous when she seemed melancholy or reserved during this time. I didn't want her to suddenly change her mind and decide she didn't want to be married anymore. But I knew I had to trust her and trust our love.

Lauren

For me, the biggest adjustment was learning how to share space. I had never lived with a man before. I was so used to having my own space and spending time alone. That's how I operate. That's how I work and tap into my creativity. People often talk about my bubbly personality, but the truth is I'm an introvert, so I need to be able to decompress in private, talk to myself out loud, and just have a space where I feel safe, in my own right, with myself, outside of being married. Cameron worried that he was doing something wrong when the truth is, he was doing everything right, showing love and support and giving me the space I needed to find my place within the framework of our marriage and new life together.

Cameron

I learned early in our relationship that Lauren feared being married would mean giving up part of who she is or making sacrifices that would infringe upon her freedom and individuality. I wanted to assure her that that wasn't going to be the case. For any married couple, it's important to learn how to give each other space. Regardless of how much you love each other and enjoy spending time together, it's vital that you maintain your own passions and personal projects. I struggled with accepting Lauren's need for space at first because when we had first gotten together we couldn't keep our hands off each other. After we got married and were settling into new daily routines, I wanted to maintain that level of affection. When I felt like there was less physical intimacy between us, I would ask her what was wrong and she would tell me nothing was wrong; she just needed space. We had variations of that conversation so many times, I often worried she might get fed up with me for good. It took considerable patience on both our parts to hear where we were both coming from and make adjustments for each other.

Over time, I started to read Lauren better and better. If we were in each other's space for too long, she would start to retreat, becoming less talkative and excited. In the beginning, I would think, *What did I do wrong? What can I do differently?* But then I learned to read the cues and recognize when she needed to recharge her batteries, like all introverts need to do, myself included. Not enough alone time can make me irritable too. In those moments, I learned to take a step back and focus on my own projects. When I give Lauren the space she needs, she is usually much more affectionate and happy. It is a lesson I still have to remind myself of from time to time.

Lauren

But, let's not forget about the fun and romance! The way Cam and I are talking, you might think our first months together were filled with simmering tension. But we had a ton of good times during that period. As Cameron alluded to earlier, our relationship happened in reverse: we fell in love and got married and *then* we started to date. So we made a point of going on a lot of dates in that year before the premiere of *Love Is Blind*. At that time, no one from the public knew who we were, so Production hadn't restricted where we could go or who we could talk to, though of course we had to conceal how we met. When people asked—and the fact that we're an intriguing-looking couple means they did so a lot—we usually said we had been set up on a blind date and left it at that.

Obviously, Cam and I had gotten to know each other extremely well in the pods and throughout the rest of filming. But the conversations on those post-show dates had a different quality to them. We could be completely unfiltered and get to know each other on an even deeper level.

Not surprisingly, Cameron was *very* good at planning dates. One that stands out was an evening at the Atlanta Botanical Garden. I'm a big fan of all things old Hollywood, the golden age of moviemaking, with stars like Audrey Hepburn, Dorothy Dandridge, and Sydney Poitier. Cam found out that the Garden was doing a special 1950s Hollywood-themed Valentine's Day event. This was our first V-day together, so he surprised me with tickets. We got all dolled up and spent a magical night together. There were lights strung throughout the trees, which made the entire landscape sparkle. The fireplaces were all blazing, there was live music and drinks. It was a thousand times more magical than anything we experienced on the set of *Love Is Blind*, because it was completely ours.

Cameron

Those date nights we had as newlyweds will always have a special place in my heart. I always feel a burst of excitement when we discover something new that we like to do together. In any relationship, I think there's a tendency to focus on points of contrast. Don't get me wrong, Lauren and I do have our share of those—I will never enjoy watching *Sex and the City*, for example. But I think what helps make a marriage strong is constantly finding things that you like to do together, especially experiences that are new to you both. As individuals, we're constantly evolving, and so our interests continue to change. It's amazing to try new things together and experience the excitement of something unexpected as a couple.

Hiking has become one of our favorite shared activities. The perfect day for us would start with a long hike outside Atlanta, maybe along the Chattahoochee River or up Stone Mountain, followed by catching a movie or a play, then a romantic evening at home. We've found that multilayered dates, with a few different types of activities, are the dates we remember the most. Lauren and I are both creatures of habit, so our first instinct is often to go with one of our old favorites, like a restaurant we both love or a park we have walked to many times in the past. We always have fun revisiting the places where we have already formed fond memories, but we make an effort to have novel experiences as well. For instance, we finally went on the Ferris wheel date we talked about in the pods! Some of our most memorable dates include picking out our first real Christmas tree together, going to see *Wicked* at the Fox Theatre, and driving to Alabama to pick up baby Sparx.

Like many couples, there have been times we found ourselves having dinner in front of the television. While those quiet nights at home are special and necessary, the times we have stepped outside our routine are the times that remain in our minds the most. If things don't go as well as we hoped, at least we have a story to tell of our misadventure.

Lauren

Cameron and I were both open to new individual experiences as well, which added to the texture and depth of our relationship. I started daily meditations, for example. It became part of my morning routine. I would get up and take my tea outside and then do a ten-minute meditation. Especially when I was feeling stressed out by life, meditation and prayer was the best way to find my chi and return to center.

I also became more focused on journaling. My thoughts were all over the place during those initial months of marriage. The act of sitting down and putting pen to paper helped me sort through the groundswell of emotions. I was so used to living on my own and being completely self-sufficient. It was hard for me to let go and realize, *Okay, I have a partner now. I don't have to do everything on my own.*

Cameron

After we got married, I was careful to avoid being complacent in our relationship, as I had witnessed myself become too comfortable in past relationships. The early phase of a relationship is such a rush. In my experience, after you settle into a routine and start seeing your partner every day, the relationship may feel less exciting and you may stop appreciating your partner and all the things they do as much. One way I countered this was by coming up with fresh date ideas, as I mentioned earlier. I also learned to jot down a list of questions I wanted to ask Lauren later, so when I got the chance to talk to her I knew what I wanted to learn about her. Lauren and I used this simple idea during our experience in the pods, but there was an opportunity to probe even deeper now that we were husband and wife. There's always going to be more to learn about a person and there's always going to be more ways in which to grow your connection. It worked for me in the pods and it continues to be a great way to get to know her more each day.

Lauren and I are planners. We thrive on to-do lists and setting goals. Each Monday, we have family meetings where we go over what we have to accomplish over the upcoming week. We usually take these meetings lying in bed with a cup of coffee or tea and a notebook.

In one such meeting, I asked, "What do you see as your immediate goals in the next few months?"

"I want to have a creative space for us to work outside of the house," she replied. We talked about how having a workplace outside the house, instead of both of us working out of our home offices, would help us have a better home life/work balance. We talked about what we both needed in a studio space for our creative pursuits, how we would utilize it to give each other room to work, and the steps we would need to take to make it a reality. It didn't happen overnight, but we eventually found a studio space in the city. But I don't want to jump too far ahead, so we'll save that story for later in the book.

Lauren

Every conversation we had during this time, every hike we took, and every date night we went on helped me through the transition from *Love Is Blind* into married life with Cameron. It was a struggle in the beginning. Without the cameras rolling and the constant buzz of the set, there was suddenly so much silence. And I ended up inside my head a lot, which wasn't healthy for me or for the relationship.

Getting to know each other on a deeper level lifted me over the hump of uncertainty. Something clicked inside of me. I thought to myself, *You know what, Cameron is right. We're married. We're partners. I'm my own person, but that doesn't mean I have to struggle alone.* From that point forward, I was able to relax into my marriage and truly begin the process of creating a life with Cameron. There were no cameras rolling, but that moment of acceptance is more vivid in my mind than any scene from the show.

Great Dates

Variety is the spice of life, especially when it comes to keeping your relationship exciting. There is nothing wrong with going on familiar dates you both love, but it is also important to try new things and get outside your comfort zone. Here are a few of our favorite things to do:

Set a romantic scene at home. We are all spending more time at home these days, which is why it's more important than ever to be creative with your home date nights. Transform the house into a romantic setting by placing candles, flowers, and any other decorations you like throughout. Put on your favorite sexy playlist and outfit. It's also a good idea to take care of the chores and whatever other responsibilities are lingering so you both can focus on each other. Find a recipe that you and your partner have never made before and surprise them with it. The key is to remove reminders of work and responsibilities for the night and to bring an air of excitement to your routine home environment.

Attend the theater. Not long after we married, we caught the show *Wicked* at the Fox Theatre in Atlanta. It's an amazing musical. We were both in total awe of the performance. The most surreal part to come of it happened a year later when one of the lead actresses reached out after we posted a picture of ourselves at the theater on Instagram. She replied: "Oh my God, I'm a huge fan of *Love Is Blind* and of you guys" to our post. That made that particular date night extra special.

Check out an exhibit. We both look to art for inspiration, so museum visits are a favorite way to spend an afternoon or evening, followed by dinner out and a walk around the neighborhood (we love compound dates with a few different parts). Around the time of our one-year anniversary, we caught the Virgil Abloh exhibit at the High Museum of Art in Atlanta. He's a Black artist from Chicago who became creative director of menswear at Louis Vuitton back in 2018. However, our favorite work of art at the High Museum was a painting of a mischievous-looking woman eating grapes we affectionately referred to as "Grape Lady." She makes us both laugh whenever we see her grin and takes us back to that timeless date.

Go small. We're all for dates that challenge and inspire, but sometimes the simpler things in life are the best. When the weather is nice, we'll pick up a couple sandwiches from the local Subway and head to the park for a laid-back picnic. Spending time together doesn't have to be elaborate. In fact, some of our best, most meaningful conversations have taken place during these casual outings. It's all about creating space for you and your partner to be together, away from the distractions of daily life.

Do some research. You don't have to figure everything out on your own! Some of our dates came from watching restaurant reviews on TikTok and reading "Top 10 Romantic Date Spots in Atlanta" articles online. It also helps to keep a list of places you would like to go and activities you would like to do, so when date night is approaching you don't have to scramble for ideas. Also check out apps like Groupon, which can spark some great date ideas and give you a discount too.

Try something new. Some of our most memorable dates came from putting in the extra effort to plan something we had never done together. Here are some of our favorite dates:

- Going to the Atlanta Botanical Garden on Valentine's Day during their old Hollywood theme
- Hiking in the Garden of the Gods in Colorado for Cameron's birthday
- Taking Lauren to the shooting range for the first time
- Going on a cabin retreat in rural Georgia
- Seeing *Wicked* at the Fox Theatre
- Going to Dad's Garage (a comedy club in Atlanta)

chapter sixteen

THE ART OF COMPROMISE

Lauren

There are two kinds of people in this world: those who love dogs and everybody else. I have always been a dog lover, going all the way back to my poodle, Layjay, one of my first pets growing up. We kept her nails painted red to match her perfectly manicured cut. Or Max, our sweet golden retriever who followed me around like a shadow.

As an adult, I'm still obsessed with dogs, but more than that, they're a huge source of psychological comfort. As you can probably tell by now, I have a lot of anxiety in my life. Work situations, home situations, social situations, all of the above. One of the tough things about anxiety is that it can be triggered by anything. I'm also very cerebral, so it's easy for me to feel overwhelmed. My heart starts pounding so hard that it feels like it's going to beat right out of my chest. I'll feel short of breath and my skin will break out in a cold sweat. Basically, your classic anxiety attack.

During my early twenties, I had a Pomeranian named Pepe. He was my bosom buddy. We'd go to parties together and out for drinks with friends. But besides being great company, he was also an incredible comfort when anxiety attacked. I'd sit on the couch and take him in my arms and my heart rate would drop immediately. My lungs would fill with air and my clammy hands would dry out again.

I didn't tell any of this to Cam the first time the topic of pets came up in the pods. But I did admit to being a bit of a dog person. I couldn't see his expression, of course, but I could practically feel the grimace through the wall between us.

Cameron

It's fair to say, I am not a dog person, or at least I wasn't for most of my life. Not by a long shot. And it's not that I didn't like dogs; I just never wanted to live with them. I actually grew up with dogs. We had two English setters, Woody and Sadie, for most of my childhood and teenage years. My dad worked as a hunting guide and trained the dogs to be experts in pointing out ruffed grouse and woodcock. As renowned as they were for their hunting prowess, the dogs were a constant headache. They barked at the slightest disturbance, they slobbered over everything, and their fine white hair was literally everywhere. No amount of vacuuming could tame the spread of hair. I vowed I would never again live in a household with a dog.

My disdain for dog ownership was well known within the family. My mom was always bothered by the fact that I didn't want to have a dog and would often prod me by asking, "Well, what about a [insert dog breed here]? They're nice and they don't shed." At one particular family dinner she asked, "What if your girlfriend or your wife wants to get a dog?"

"Then she's got to go."

"Cameron, you can't be serious."

I meant what I said. Especially post-college, when I was living on my own, dogs were a deal breaker in my search for love. I know it sounds harsh, but I figured there were so many eligible women out there who weren't dog people that I could afford to be picky on this one point.

Then came Lauren.

I remember the moment in the pods when she professed her love for dogs. In the past, I would have started crossing the person off my list at the mention of a dog. But with Lauren it was different: I could already envision the two of us chasing the dog around the living room and going on long walks with him. We started talking about what it would be like to raise a dog from a puppy together and joked about how much of a troublemaker he would be. One pod date, Lauren asked me what we would name the dog. I racked my brain for something to fit the high-energy dog we imagined.

"How about Sparx?" I offered.

"Ooohhh, like the sparks between us!" she said excitedly.

"Exactly."

Lauren

When it comes to love, "compromise" can feel like a dirty word. It's easy for one person in the relationship to feel like they're settling for something they don't really want just because they're tired of arguing. But true compromise isn't about giving in. It's about finding common ground through empathy and communication.

In the case of the dog, there was no "it's the dog way or the highway" ultimatum. We had a bunch of conversations.

"I can't stand all the hair," Cameron said during one of our early dates in the pod. "The thought of constantly vacuuming it up drives me crazy."

"Yeah, that can be pretty disgusting," I empathized. "But you know, there are a lot of breeds out there that don't shed a lot, especially if you keep up with the grooming." I didn't push too hard, but I could sense that he was starting to warm to the idea.

A few weeks later, after we left the set of *Love Is Blind* for good, we were walking through our neighborhood in Atlanta when the topic came up again. I shared more about the calming, anxiety-fighting effects dogs have always had on me.

Cameron appreciated my honesty and added this perspective of dog ownership to his list of pros and cons. He was becoming even more open to the thought of becoming a puppy parent.

"I really don't want the decision to be just about me and my needs. I won't be happy having a dog if I know it's making you unhappy," I confessed to Cameron.

"Lauren, I want to get a dog," he said. "For us."

And that's how baby Sparx, the most adorable, precocious Airedale puppy that ever was, came into our lives.

Cameron

Sparx has definitely made a dog lover out of me. I can't imagine not having him as part of the family now, even if he chews everything in sight and eats whole bars of soap like during Thanksgiving 2019.

But in all seriousness, Sparx was one of our first lessons in compromise, one that paved the way for larger, more serious challenges in the relationship. I think one of the biggest challenges for me early on had to do with Lauren's apartment. As you may have already noted, Lauren was extremely reluctant to give up her apartment after we wrapped *Love Is Blind.*

We were hiking up Stone Mountain when the subject first came up.

"How would you feel about me keeping my apartment?" she asked.

"Well, I'm not sure why you would want to do that," I responded. "We have the house, which belongs to both of us now. I want this house to be your home. I want you to feel completely comfortable there."

"I know, Cameron," she said. "But I've never lived with a man before, let alone been married to one and moved into his house. It's just a lot to process all at once."

My worst fears and insecurities started rising to the surface. I was afraid this was a sign she was having second thoughts about our marriage and was looking for an escape route. I tried to conceal my discomfort, but I've never been able to hide my emotions; my face is an open book.

"It's not a reflection of you," Lauren said reassuringly. "It's a reflection of the fact that I need my alone time sometimes. And that this apartment really means a lot to me."

"I know your apartment is very special to you," I said. "And ultimately it's your apartment, so I can't tell you what to do with it. I just don't want you to have second thoughts about anything."

"Well, let's just think about it for now, okay?" she said.

And suddenly, getting a dog together did not seem like a big deal by comparison.

I thought about what Lauren holding on to her apartment meant as another week passed. I was having a hard time moving beyond my fear that she might be having second thoughts. At the same time, I knew I had to trust her if we were going to have a successful relationship and that I must not let my insecurities get in the way of that. I also tried my best to put myself in her shoes and consider how big of a transition this was for her. I wanted her to be happy and I realized anything I did that would limit her freedom would only drive her further away from me. When I felt like I had gathered up my thoughts, I broached the subject again. We were having dinner at Nuevo Laredo Cantina, one of our favorite restaurants in Atlanta.

"So I want to talk about your apartment again," I began. "I know how important your own space is for your creativity. I also know that your apartment represents your freedom and independence. I get all that. And yet, I can't help but think that you also want to hold on to your apartment in the event you decide to change your mind about being married to me. I'm afraid that the more time you spend there, the less you are going to want to spend time with me. But I also realize this is what you need to be happy and I am willing to do what it takes to make you happy, even if that means spending less time together."

As close as Lauren and I had become by that point, it was still difficult to admit my insecurities that openly. But I knew that the only way we were going to come to any resolution was to lay all our cards on the table.

Lauren

There's a time to talk in a relationship and there's a time to listen. Sitting with Cameron that night at the restaurant, I knew it was a time for me to listen. Sure, there was a part of me that wanted to tell Cameron I thought he was being ridiculous! Of course I'm not going to hide out in my apartment! But that would have invalidated his feelings.

Instead, I asked more questions to understand where these feelings were coming from. Cameron talked about some of his past relationships that had ended badly. In one case, he and his girlfriend had to be physically apart for long stretches of time and that led to a kind of emotional separation. Another girlfriend had been unfaithful to him during a prolonged separation and that created a lot of trust issues.

"Babe, I feel your pain because I've experienced that myself," I said, referring to the boyfriend in college who cheated on me. "But I promise you, that's not what this is about. I will be loyal to our marriage."

"I know that," Cameron responded. "In my heart I know you would never be unfaithful. Just as I know I could never ever be unfaithful to you. But it's still hard for me to understand why you are struggling with letting go of the apartment."

We were at an impasse. And yet it didn't feel hopeless because we were being honest about our feelings and respectful of each other's position.

Cameron

That is a critical point about compromise: it doesn't just happen. You need to be patient. When there's an issue in a relationship, it's easy to feel like you're running around in circles, like the situation is never going to change. It's important to take a step back and assess if any progress has been made, however small or incremental. Some issues take a long time to resolve. You have to ask yourself if you have the patience and the compassion to see the compromise through to the end. You also have to ask yourself if you can live with this issue in the event it is never resolved.

You may find that there are times when one or both of you cannot and should not compromise. For instance, if your partner gets a dream job offer that will require them to move to another state, you cannot expect them to pass on that opportunity because it will make spending time together more difficult. The compromise should not involve sacrificing aspects of one's identity to satisfy one's partner. Compromise is about the willingness to listen and understand where your partner is coming from. You must decide together how best to proceed, even if the solution you arrive at is to simply accept a suboptimal situation, like having to travel to spend time with your partner. To put it more succinctly, compromise on the things you can (i.e., things that won't breed resentment), and where you can't, seek to understand and respect each other.

Dinner at Nuevo Laredo Cantina that night did not end our discussion about Lauren giving up her apartment. But we moved the issue forward by practicing honesty, compassion, and respect.

I continued to express that I accepted her keeping her apartment, even if I was hesitant at first. In the weeks that followed, she continued to take day trips to her apartment, even spending the night there on occasion. I missed her when she was away, but it didn't scare me anymore because I realized that I needed to trust her. I came to accept that she was just getting the one-on-one time with herself that she needed, because that's how she had lived her life for the past thirty-three years.

This continued for a good two or three months. Then one afternoon I came home from the gym. Lauren was on her laptop at the kitchen table.

"Hey, babe, what are you up to?" I asked.

"Writing an email to my property manager," she said.

"Oh yeah, what for?"

"For the apartment," she said. "I've decided I'm not going to renew my lease."

I went over and wrapped her in my arms.

"I love you," I said.

"I love you too," she said, then added, "Now we have to find a studio space for us to work out of."

"You got it, baby!"

Where to Draw the Line

While compromise is crucial to a relationship, there are certain actions and behaviors that are too toxic for any healthy relationship to survive. Of course, it's important to forgive, but if your partner does any of the following over and over again, you probably need to walk away. In some cases, you might even need to get out of the relationship after one strike.

Infidelity. Relationships are built on trust. If your partner isn't faithful to you, that's an automatic deal breaker. Yes, there are couples who work through the issue if it happens once, but even then, the damage to the foundation of the relationship may be too much to repair. And if the person you love is continuously carrying on behind your back, protect yourself by ending things. In short, stay true to each other or move on.

Abuse. Whether it's physical or emotional, abuse in a relationship is completely unacceptable. We've both experienced it to varying degrees in past relationships. It often starts small, with minor shows of contempt, maybe a cruel joke or put-down. But slowly over time, the insults or attacks become increasingly hurtful. And it's easy for the victim to feel like it's their fault, like they somehow deserve the abuse. There is someone out there who will love you better than that.

Addiction. This is a tough one, because substance abuse is so prevalent in our society. Yes, you should show compassion if you're in love with someone who has a drug or alcohol problem. But if they refuse to get help, there will come a point when you will have to extricate yourself. This is something else that we've experienced firsthand. In our experience, the addiction creates so much chaos that it becomes impossible to establish long-term goals as a couple, especially when *you're* willing to compromise but your partner doesn't seem to be.

Unwillingness to compromise. As discussed, compromise is a critical part of a relationship that is founded on mutual respect and understanding. If you and your partner respect each other and both seek to understand where the other is coming from, chances are you will be able to come to a solution that you both deem fair. For instance, if you are deciding whether to spend the holiday with your partner's family or your own, a reasonable compromise might be to alternate where you go each year or to try to visit both families for a few days each. However, if your partner is totally unwilling to meet you halfway, that's a serious red flag. Try to have a conversation to figure out their unwillingness to hear you out and to try to find a middle ground. Of course, neither of you should compromise in situations that require you to sacrifice your self-identity or that would breed resentment for each other. Even in the most challenging situations, however, both people need to feel heard and respected, even if there isn't a satisfying solution to your current dilemma.

chapter seventeen

RACE RELATIONSHIPS

Lauren

Even though Cameron and I don't wake up every morning and remind each other that we're an interracial couple, anyone who watched the show might actually think it's all we talk about (and they'll definitely think it's the only thing on my dad's mind!). The truth is that our marriage, like any relationship, is incredibly complex and multilayered. Race is one of the layers. It's never our main focus, but we both understand that it is something that must be addressed at times, no matter how uncomfortable that may be.

I think back to the summer of 2020, at the height of the Black Lives Matter movement. It felt like every day there was more horrifying news, from George Floyd to Breonna Taylor to riots in the streets around the country. It was hard for me to process it all, despite the fact that when you grow up Black in America, race is something you talk about from the beginning. Black parents pretty much train their children from as young as five and six on how to interact with the police. We're told what to say and what not to say, because if you say the wrong thing the situation can get dangerous or even deadly. I was disgusted by the constant stream of racial injustices but I wasn't surprised. However, that didn't make them any easier to digest mentally and emotionally.

By that point, *Love Is Blind* had been streaming for almost six months, so Cameron and I were in the public eye as a mixed-race couple. I remember logging on to Instagram one morning and finding a barrage of DMs.

"Lauren, you're a Black woman," one of them said. "You have a platform. You need to be speaking out against this."

It was difficult because I was still trying to process what was happening in my own mind as a Black woman, let alone as a leader for all Black women around the world. I went for a walk around the neighborhood to try to collect myself and organize my thoughts. But no matter how hard I tried, I couldn't escape the great weight on my chest, the anger and frustration welling up inside of me.

I came back home and collapsed in a heap in the middle of our bedroom floor and just started to sob uncontrollably. Prior to marriage, that's the type of moment I would have by myself. I wouldn't even let my parents see me in that state. But I couldn't keep it from Cameron. He came into the room and immediately tried to comfort me.

"I don't want you to hold me," I said. "I need you to give me this space to cry." It was hard to say that to him, because I knew he was only trying to help. But the solitude was necessary. After a few minutes I settled down and we talked some more.

"I love how supportive you are," I told Cameron. "But you will never understand what this feels like. And I can't explain it to you.

You'll never know what it's like to be a Black person in this country and experience all of the pain that is happening in our minds and hearts right now. Where I'm at mentally and where you're at mentally, there is just so much space between us. You will never feel how I feel. What you can do, though, is listen."

That was probably the hardest conversation of our entire relationship. Because Cameron always wants to fix things. And in that moment, he realized that this wasn't something he could fix. But he was willing to listen. And that was the support I needed.

Cameron

My understanding of race and ethnicity has been evolving since I was a child, and it's a process that continues today. There will always be more for me to learn, and I will never know what it is like to be Black. I can only ever experience what it is like to be me, not anyone else, and especially not someone who has experienced systemic prejudice. I am grateful for the opportunity to continue learning how to be the most supportive husband I can be to Lauren as well as the best ally I can be.

Growing up in rural Maine, I didn't see many people who looked different than me. Nonetheless, I was aware that there are people of all different races, ethnicities, nationalities, sexual orientations, religions, and cultures. My mom also helped start an international program at my town's high school, Lee Academy, that brought in students from all over the world. This exposure to people of different backgrounds in my adolescent years onward was invaluable to me, as it opened my eyes to the broader world.

Growing up, I had heard people promoting stereotypes like "all Black people like hip-hop and play basketball," but I reasoned that stereotypes could not be universally true. I reflected on my own Maine culture and how I often felt like an outsider—I wasn't crazy about hunting and fishing, I didn't care for country music, and I didn't want to work in the lumber industry. If I could be so different from the stereotype of a Mainer, then it made sense that people from other backgrounds did not have to conform to the expectations ascribed to them. The more I thought about it, the more intuitive it seemed that at the end of the day, we are all just people, created from the same genetic material and with the same basic needs and desires. We all want to be treated fairly and to be comfortable in our daily lives, have the freedom to pursue our dreams, to be respected by others, and to have fun.

Because this all seemed obvious to me, I didn't understand why everyone else hadn't reached the same conclusion. As I got older and observed how people treat others who are different from them, I started to realize that prejudice takes on many forms. I also learned that subtle racism is no less painful or wrong. For example, my best friend in college was an Indian American guy. People sometimes compared him to Kevin G, the Indian character from *Mean Girls*, because he liked to rap and the character in the movie also rapped. Sometimes they would compare him to Kumar from *Harold & Kumar* simply on the grounds that they both have an Indian background. Even though my friend always laughed it off when people called him Kevin G or Kumar, I could tell from his body language and comments he made to me later that it hurt his feelings to be reduced to a character. In those moments, I recognized that it was wrong and hurtful for people to call him those names, and often called people out for it. But looking back, I'm ashamed that I didn't do more. I was starting to see racism in action more and more, but it was still just the beginning of my awareness.

It wasn't until grad school, when I left Maine for the majority Black city of Atlanta, that I started to get educated on the systemic and life-threatening ways Black people are still discriminated against. The statistics are there to back that up, including the fact that Black people are three to four times more likely to be killed by police than white people, according to a 2020 study by researchers from Harvard T.H. Chan School of Public Health.

I remember having a conversation in 2014 with a Black woman I was dating about the recent shootings of Eric Garner and Michael Brown. This was during my philosophy grad program and I had gotten into the habit of playing devil's advocate, even if I agreed with the person I was talking to. And so I took the position that, because I didn't know all the context of what transpired leading up to the shooting, I could not say for sure whether it was justified or not. I didn't realize at the time that it was my white privilege that enabled me to take such a callous position, even if I was taking it for the sake of discussion. My white privilege had allowed me to believe that law enforcement could almost always be trusted. I did not think about how it must have felt for my girlfriend to hear her partner's seeming lack of empathy. I did not fully consider the pain, fear, and exhaustion that comes from watching another member of your community killed by the people sworn to protect you. I am embarrassed by my former ignorance and insensitivity, but I bring this story up because I think it highlights a common failure of people with privilege—a rank ignorance of the mistreatment of people subject to systemic prejudice, resulting in a lack of compassion.

Lauren

The willingness to listen is extremely important in an interracial relationship, but so is the willingness to teach. Oftentimes, one person in the relationship will get frustrated because they feel like the other person doesn't understand them. Or they think the fact that their partner has to be taught something makes them ignorant. But it may simply be that they just aren't informed.

This reminds me of a story from one of my modeling gigs after *Love Is Blind* was filmed but before the show had come out. I wasn't advertising the fact that I was married, but another model on the shoot was an old friend, so I confided in her that I'd recently tied the knot.

"Oh really?" she said. "Let me see a picture." So I pulled out a pic of Cam.

She shared that she also was in an interracial relationship. She's white and went on to explain that she'd been dating a Black man. "But I don't think it's going to work out because he's constantly getting upset at me for not knowing things about Black culture."

"Okay, that is not good," I told her.

A few weeks later, I ran into the friend at another shoot. "How's your boyfriend?" I asked.

"What boyfriend?" she answered, rolling her eyes. The lesson is a hard one for many mixed-race couples because, let's face it, there are undeniable differences between Black and white cultures.

Take the standout scene from *Love Is Blind*, where I'm shown wearing a bonnet to bed, like a lot of Black women do. Cameron had dated Black women previously, so he was no stranger to the bonnet life. But for many mixed-race couples, that would have been a highly teachable moment, and not all of them would be able to navigate it.

On this point, the show also made a lot out of the fact that I'd never dated a white man before Cameron. It wasn't for lack of interest. Throughout my life, I've had crushes on men who are white, whether a celebrity on television or someone from real life. There would be times I would be giving a Caucasian man the eyes, to no avail. It got to the point where I started to think, *Do I look mean or intimidating? Do I have resting bitch face or something? I'm like the nicest person ever!*

Cameron

Even on set, I had so many conversations with guys about their hesitancy to date outside their race. They talked about the fact that they were interested in other races, but their parents or peers had convinced them that mixed-race dating was not a normal or acceptable thing to do. It was sad to hear some guys talk about having an initial connection with a woman on the other side of the wall, then casually dismiss the possibility of a relationship on account of her ethnicity. I felt like these guys were sparking up a conversation with me because they knew Lauren and I were progressing forward and they wanted to see how I was able to do so.

My advice to my fellow cast members back then is the same advice I have now: You need to do what is best for you, not your family and peers. It's not easy to date someone when people close to you look down upon your relationship, but you need to be brave and live how you want to live. You will inevitably face challenges as an interracial couple, whether uncomfortable conversations about racial inequality, differences in culture, or criticism from the outside world. It may be easier to take the path of least resistance and date someone who neatly fits with who society and your social circle believe is an appropriate match for you. But in limiting yourself in this way, you may be missing out on the person who could make you your happiest self and elevate your life in ways no one else can.

Lauren

Cameron and I know it's still a tough road ahead. When we talk about raising children, for example, we know that they'll be viewed as Black by most of society, so we'll need to have hard conversations with them. We know that for some aspects of those conversations, Cam won't be able to speak from experience. But he is learning to deal with prejudice against our relationship, which we openly have encountered living in Georgia. I remember the first time this happened. We were walking down the street in our neighborhood when an agitated homeless man who was Black gave us the stink eye and started spewing animosity. "Look at you with that white man," he scoffed. We just kept walking and ignored him but it was still irritating.

It can get even worse online. Shortly after the *LIB* premiere, some rando sent me a DM calling me a bed wench, which is a really hurtful term used in the Black community, referring back to slavery, when enslaved Black women would have to sleep with their masters in exchange for privileges or higher status among the other enslaved women. I was able to brush it off because it's such an ignorant thing to label me and my love story, but also because the overwhelming majority of comments we get on social media are full of love and support.

Cameron

I get the occasional negative message too. Every once in a while, some troll will tell me I should be with a white woman or disparage our relationship in general, but those messages are now thankfully rare. The rest of the time, the engagement from followers is totally supportive. Most messages are: "You guys look great together," "Y'all are such a beautiful couple," or "We love to see a couple thriving like y'all." I know we have a long, long way to go in our society toward racial equality, but I see those messages as a positive sign of progress. That said, I have also noticed that whenever Lauren and I post about systemic racism or Black Lives Matter on social media we see a sharp decline in followers that day, sometimes even a couple thousand. This further emphasizes how unwilling some people still are to address prejudice in our country and how much work is left to be done.

A significant amount of the fan outreach we receive, especially on social media, is people seeking advice about their own interracial relationship. During the 2020 protests following the deaths of Breonna Taylor, George Floyd, and Ahmaud Arbery, a guy in a mixed-race relationship reached out to me on Instagram. "Obviously, there's a lot going on in the world right now with respect to the treatment of Black people," he wrote. "My partner's very upset. I want to communicate with her but I'm not sure exactly how to do that. How should I talk to her about what's going on in the world? What should I do?"

I don't pretend to be an authority on race relations. But I can share what's worked for me. There's a quote I like that goes something like, "Any act done out of compassion can't be wrong." When people come to me with these questions, I always start with that. If you can begin from a place of empathy and actively listen to your partner, you will have taken a critical first step toward supporting them. You have to be willing to have the hard conversations and to be vulnerable enough to admit when you have benefited from privilege to yourself and your partner. It is important that you talk to your partner about how you can best support them and it is okay to ask them questions about things you do not understand, but you also have to realize that you cannot depend on your partner to educate you on everything you should know about the prejudice they are experiencing. If your partner is suffering because of a loss they experienced within their community, they will likely not have the mental or emotional bandwidth to answer all your questions, so it is best to seek out online resources to educate yourself. One resource I have found helpful is "A Growing List of Resources for the Movement for Black Lives," which includes links to literature on allyship, petitions, protest information, charitable organizations, and many more ways to get involved. In sum, if you and your partner build your relationship on shared compassion and respect for each other, you can make the relationship work, regardless of race, religion, or any other differences.

Lauren's Last Words

When I think back over my relationship with Cameron in the context of race, these two stories really stand out, because they taught me so much about myself.

Find strength in vulnerability. On the second or third night of our proposal-moon on the show, we were hanging out in the resort. I was lying on the bed and Cameron was milling about the room. All of a sudden, I started to cry.

"What's wrong?" Cameron asked gently.

"I was thinking about our children and the struggles they might endure being mixed race. Will they be treated poorly? Will they get teased on the playground?" I felt sorry for them and it filled me with so much sadness. Cameron held me for a few minutes.

"It's going to be okay," he said finally. "We are going to raise them together. They are going to be loved and they are going to know both cultures. And that's going to make them that much more amazing."

We looked at each other for a solid few minutes.

"You know what?" I said. "You're right. And this is the last time I will ever cry about that." And I've kept my word.

Show tolerance in certain situations. One time during a visit with Cam's family, I had just gotten new braids. One of his older relatives asked if he could touch my hair. This is a pretty sensitive area in the Black community, because it feeds into the idea that Black hair is "other," this crazy intriguing thing that is so "out of this world." Historically, Black people would travel around the country in these sideshows and be paraded around because of their "strange" features . . . abnormal hair and different bodies. So needless to say, a lot of Black people are sensitive when it comes to those things.

My instinct was to say, "Hell, no! You can't touch my hair!" Instead, I thought to myself, *You know what, this is a teaching moment.* I let him touch one of the braids and then I asked if he had any questions. I also found a way to gently recommend that he not go around asking random Black women if he can touch their hair.

It was one of those moments that could have gone any number of ways. I could have gotten angry. I could have made Cam and his family feel bad. But I made the decision that we are family and it was a chance to teach and to learn. At the end of the day, I think we have to realize that we're all just finding our way through the world. As long as there's respect within the relationship, it's okay to show a little extra kindness and vulnerability.

chapter eighteen

TRYING ON MARRIAGE ROLES

Cameron

A month or so after the wedding, as Lauren and I were starting our life together back in Atlanta, I came home late one night to a quiet house. I would usually find Lauren hanging out in the kitchen or her office, but she wasn't anywhere to be found. I made my way upstairs to the bedroom. As I got closer to the door, I heard the sound of muffled crying.

This wasn't long after her aunt had passed away, so I thought maybe Lauren was grieving. I walked into the bedroom, sat down beside her on the bed, and rubbed her back gently.

"What's going on, babe?" I asked. "Tell me what happened."

I looked over at her laptop on the bed. The web browser was open to an article about the evolution of marriage over time. There was a chart showing the various phases—the passion/honeymoon phase, the realization/acceptance phase, the period of rebellion, and so on. At the end, the chart split into two directions: the completion phase for couples who make it and the divorce phase for those who don't.

"I don't want to get divorced," Lauren said, her sobs slowly subsiding.

"Who said anything about divorce?" I asked. We talked about divorce often during *Love Is Blind*, but it hadn't come up since then. Even though the divorce rate is dropping in the US, nearly half of all marriages still end in divorce, according to the American Psychological Association. Lauren and I were aware of the statistics, but we were also clear on the point that divorce would never be an option for us. We talked about the sanctity of marriage and the idea that when you take the vows, it truly is till death do you part.

My parents constantly reminded me how much work marriage is, even with the right partner. Through nearly four decades of marriage, they've had their share of disagreements and bickering. When I was a child, it used to scare me to see them get into an argument, but as I got older I saw how those arguments cooled fairly quickly and ended in resolutions. At the end of the day, my parents were always on the same team. I revered their mutual respect for each other. My sister and I never had to worry that our mom and dad might not stay together. I saw their relationship grow stronger over the years, especially when faced with a challenge, like when my mom was diagnosed with breast cancer in 2012. I wanted that same stability and support for my kids, and I know Lauren did as well.

Lauren

When I stumbled onto that article about the phases of marriage that night, it shook my confidence. I had a momentary freak-out.

But then Cameron was beside me, reminding me of all the promises we had made.

"I know you're worried that your parents' fate will be repeated in us," he said. "But that doesn't have to be the case. Ultimately, we are responsible for creating our own destiny. It's up to us, and whether we're willing to put in the work."

"One hundred percent, Cameron," I said. We weren't about to abandon the passion of the honeymoon phase, but in that moment I felt us crossing over to the reality of marriage. Now we had to figure out what the roles of husband and wife would be like for us.

Cameron

Our society puts so much focus on everything leading up to marriage—the wedding planning, the bridal shower, the bachelor party, and the honeymoon to follow. There does not seem to be nearly as much attention paid to life after the wedding, specifically the pragmatic ways in which married couples can live in harmony after tying the knot. Yes, there are resources out there that aim to guide couples through married life, whether it's self-help books or marriage counseling. But day-to-day matrimony is not romanticized remotely the same as all things leading up to the big day. Think how many movies have been made about couples falling in love where the climax is the wedding or the happy couple cooing over their first baby as the credits roll. Far fewer films are made about couples keeping the romance alive after years of marriage or overcoming hardships together and still continuing to thrive.

Even for couples who have been together for a long time, marriage brings with it a mental shift: You have just pledged yourself to someone for life with the understanding that you will do everything you can to help each other navigate life's perils. This person is no longer your boyfriend or girlfriend—this is your chosen life partner.

One factor I've found key to relationship health is for both parties to feel satisfied with how much the other is contributing to the relationship. If one person feels like they're doing all the work—cooking, cleaning, managing the finances, setting the social calendar—it can lead to feelings of contempt for the partner. And as with all potential sticking points in a relationship, maintaining fairness comes back to communication and compromise.

We've found it helps to have a designated time each week to bring up shared responsibilities and talk about what improvements you each would like to see. Lauren and I like to have these family meetings every Monday before launching into the next week. In these meetings we talk about shared projects we're working on (like this book!), things that need to get done around the house, and sometimes ways we can adjust to meet each other's needs.

"So what do you think is the best way to manage our finances together?" Lauren asked during one of our first meetings. We had talked about how we would split up the bills back in the pods. Lauren had noted that since she had started her business from the bottom up, she did not have as much to contribute financially. She made that point again.

"I understand," I said. "I am happy to take care of most of

our finances if you are willing to manage most of the household responsibilities."

"I still want to contribute financially as well," she said.

"I appreciate that. I think the important thing is that we're contributing equally to the relationship, even if it is not financially. I believe in you and your business, so when it takes off, we can reevaluate how we manage our money."

Lauren

Someone could have listened to that conversation between Cameron and me and thought, *Okay, traditional marriage: man provides; woman keeps the home.* And on the face of it, that's the agreement we reached. But 1) we knew the situation was temporary, and 2) it was totally out in the open. I think couples get into trouble when they slide into these roles without any discussion. Some husbands just assume their wife will handle the housework. The wife just assumes she'll quit her job once the baby comes. Neither of those things is right or wrong. But being on the same page with your partner with a clear plan can eliminate a lot of headache.

And so I did more of the work around the house. I can remember that when I was growing up, my aunt Sheila, my mom's older sister and a second mom to me, would always say things like, "You know, you have to learn how to clean the house if you ever want to find a husband. You have to learn how to cook. No man wants a dirty wife who can't feed him."

So, yes, it was easy to take on that traditional role in my

marriage. And sure enough, it didn't last more than a year. Cameron left the corporate world so that we could start a business together. Now everything is split down the middle—finances, housework, social planning, and so on. In that sense, we're a very modern couple.

But in other ways, Cam and I are quite traditional. I grew up believing that it was the man's job to protect the home and keep the family safe. That is Cameron to a tee. I was also taught that a woman needs to take care of her man. I'm happy to play that part. If I see that Cam had a hard day, I give him some extra TLC. *It needs to not be about you right now,* I'll tell myself. *Go and cheer Cameron up. Make your man happy.*

I'll do it because I want to, and also because I know Cameron will do the same thing for me the next time I need it. That's what marriage is all about.

Building Your Financial House Together

Money can be a huge headache for new couples. But talking out your finances can also be a bit of a minefield. Here are some tips that have helped us avoid any explosions:

Communicate early and often. Don't wait until after the honeymoon to discuss your attitudes about money. As the relationship becomes serious, ask each other the hard questions: How much debt are you carrying? What do you earn today? What do you hope to earn in the future? Do you invest/save?

What kind of lifestyle do you want to live? It's important to identify where your financial goals align and where they differ. If you are unwilling to talk to your partner about your financial situation, ask yourself why that is the case. Are you afraid they will judge you for your finances? Are you concerned they will try to get money from you? If you have any reason to distrust your partner with your financial information, you must address this as soon as possible, as otherwise your concerns will continue to fester.

Create a joint account. We made the decision to have one joint account for all shared expenses—the house, utilities, groceries, et cetera—once we started splitting the bills more evenly. We also maintain separate accounts for our income outside of our shared expenses so we can enjoy financial independence. If one of us wants to take the other on a date, they draw from their individual account.

Determine what you and your partner agree is fair. When one partner feels like the other is not contributing equally to the relationship, it can lead to feelings of contempt. Of course, everyone's relationship and financial situation is different, so you both have to agree on what constitutes a fair contribution. There is no one way to manage your finances and other contributions with your partner. You both do not need to contribute the exact same toward shared expenses, but you have to agree on how the distribution of household responsibilities among other tasks compensates for the imbalance.

Set goals together. We check in at least monthly on our financial goals, both short- and long-term. For example, when we made the decision to get some sort of studio space outside of the house, we had to figure out how to work that into our financial picture. Longer-term goals include things like planning for a family and mapping out an ideal retirement.

chapter nineteen

DON'T TOUCH
MY TOOTHBRUSH

Lauren

One life lesson I've learned in communicating is that "you gotta add a little sugar with your salt." That's especially true when it comes to living with Cam. I think I've made my love for him abundantly clear. He's the man of my dreams, an incredible partner through and through. Moving in, living together, we really had to adjust to each other's ways of life, including housekeeping habits. That's where the sugar comes in.

The other day I came home to a pile of dirty dishes on the kitchen counter. Cam loves to leave his dishes. If we don't eat a meal together, I can always tell what Cam had because the evidence is all over the kitchen. In this case, it looked like some spaghetti and meatballs.

In my head I'm thinking, *Cam knows I hate when he leaves these dishes; c'mon, man!* But I knew that me yelling at him about it wouldn't do either of us any good. That's the salty approach! So I found him in his office and exchanged a few pleasantries. Then, as I was leaving the room, I turned back to him and said, "Oh, and hey, babe, you know I love you, but would you mind washing your dishes next time instead of leaving them on the counter? I'm afraid we're going to get ants."

"Sure thing, love," he said. "Sorry I forgot."

Was that the last time he left a dish out? Not by a long shot. But is it happening less often? YES. Plus, the fact that I spoke up, however gently, means I won't be filled with rage and resentment every time I come home to dirty dishes.

You have to speak your mind in marriage, but a little sugar helps the medicine go down.

Cameron

She is clearly exaggerating how many dirty dishes I leave around, though there's always room for improvement, I suppose. In fairness, though, I think Lauren and I both have our strengths and our weaknesses when it comes to housekeeping. For example, my office is usually a lot cleaner than hers. But she is definitely more of a stickler in the kitchen. She is also hypervigilant about handwashing and disinfecting. Overall, we both value organization, cleanliness, and hygiene, but we sometimes differ on what constitutes each. That is why it is healthy to have conversations with your partner about your expectations and any incongruences between them.

This, of course, takes us to the notorious toothbrush scene from *Love Is Blind*. Now for me, that was twenty seconds of my life that I didn't think much about after it happened. We were having dinner and chatting about hygiene pet peeves. "You know there are people out there who will use someone else's toothbrush," Lauren said. "Do you do that?"

It was clearly a tongue-in-cheek moment between us, so I played along. "I mean, I wouldn't have a problem with it, but I'm not going to—"

"Oh my God, honey," Lauren said, cutting me off playfully. "What???"

Of course, I was just teasing Lauren—I was not actually going to use her toothbrush. And while Lauren understood I was playing with her, my own personal toothbrush-gate was born. From reenacting the scene on the Kiss Cam at Madison Square Garden to mentions of the incident across many press articles, those moments in time have continued to live on. There's even a TikTok challenge out there where couples lip-sync our conversation from the show. That moment in time has taken on a life of its own.

In all seriousness, Lauren and I are mostly on the same page with household chores, notwithstanding the occasional dirty dish. We both thrive off of getting things done and having organization in our lives. I think this goes back to the way we were raised, with our parents making us help out around the house from an early age.

We both grew up with a sense of order and discipline in the house. As a child, I felt resentful on occasion at having to chip in with the housework and abide by certain rules. The older I got, the more I appreciated the discipline my parents instilled in me. It made me feel like I had more control over my life. I had my regular chores and was also expected to help out with whatever my parents were working on, whether it was planting the garden, building their lake house, or shoveling snow.

That same attitude extends to marriage. If one person in the relationship is a total slob and the other is a neat freak, that's going to lead to conflict. If your partner needs the place to be cleaner, the smart and considerate thing to do is change your behavior. Even if you think you are clean and organized by your own standards, hear out your partner's needs and consider that more cleanliness never hurts. If you are willing to listen and make changes for your partner, they will likely be more willing to listen to your needs. Lauren and I have found that respecting each other's housekeeping requests has led to greater harmony at home and a more comfortable environment.

Lauren

I think it's a surprise for a lot of young couples how much housekeeping symbolizes in a marriage. Here's another example: I've talked a lot about how when Cameron and I first moved in together, I was stressing over my perceived loss of independence and sense of self. One way this came across was through the sharing of space in the kitchen. Or I should say lack of sharing space, because I was pretty possessive of my stuff for a long time. I would say things like, "Cam, could you hand me *my* juice." "Have you seen *my* chips?"

Cam would respond, "No, babe, that's our juice. Those are our chips."

In my mind, I would be thinking, *No! Those are mine! I bought those things for me.* Because that's how I had lived for so many years. Cam really taught me the art of sharing with your partner. It's a big part of entering into a marriage. You become a unit.

Of course, there are still things that I like to keep separate. We are very lucky to have two bathrooms, so we don't have to worry about navigating those waters. And as much as I try, I don't think I'll ever be totally comfortable washing our clothes in the same load of laundry.

I remember coming into the bedroom one day and there was Cameron folding my underwear. "Cameron, what are you doing?" I shouted. "I can fold my own intimates!"

"What's the big deal?" Cameron asked.

I knew it didn't make a lot of sense. Cam has obviously seen my panties and bras before. Still, I can't help but see underwear as personal.

"I'm sorry," I said. "I'm not used to all this personal sharing. This all feels like . . . a lot."

I think Cam heard me. For a few weeks, he focused on his own laundry. One Saturday he was about to run a load when I came over with a few of my own garments.

"Can I throw these in?" I asked. It was just a T-shirt and shorts, not my best lingerie. But it was a baby step.

Cameron

There are baby steps in a marriage and then there are huge strides forward. For us, learning to accept help from others was one of those huge strides. For instance, we had our reservations about hiring a housekeeper at first, because we were both raised to handle everything ourselves. We both find the whole cleaning process cathartic, and the thought of bringing in a housekeeper clashed with our values of self-sufficiency. Over time, however, our work schedules intensified to the point where we could not manage all of our work and household responsibilities simultaneously. We needed help.

"Let's just try it for a month," Lauren said after we finished a particularly tiresome cleaning session. "I know it's a luxury. But we work hard and are fortunate enough to be in a position where we can afford it."

I agreed. It's hard to admit, but we need help if we are going to continue to grow our business and not get burned out. It's one of the best decisions we've made to free up our time and energy. Since then, we have looked for other ways to maximize the time we have to work on our business. Though we enjoy cooking for each other, we have found using a meal prep service has saved us significant amounts of time buying groceries, thinking of meals, and cooking. Our advice to other newlyweds: try to find ways you can free up your time by working together. For example, some Sundays Lauren and I will have a meal prep day where we cook and pack all the lunches we are going to have for the week. It's fun to cook together and when you are both busy with your careers and your marriage, it's tough to find the time for other responsibilities. As my parents like to say, many hands make light work.

Household Items We Couldn't Live Without

There are a lot of products out there designed to help with hygiene and housekeeping. Some of them are a little ridiculous—pore vacuum for removing blackheads, anyone? Or how about a toaster with a built-in griddle for cooking bacon and eggs? Other gadgets do actually make your life a lot easier. Here are a few that we are excited about:

Ultrasonic toothbrush. We get a lot of compliments on our teeth, which is nice, followed by questions about oral care. First off, ultrasonic toothbrushes are a game changer. The ultrasonic vibrations are way more effective at cleaning than your standard electric toothbrush. Plus, ours has four different modes— clean, soft, whitening, and massage—plus a two-minute timer so you know you're giving your pearly whites enough TLC.

Air fryer. If you don't have one of these multipurpose countertop cookers, our advice is to run, don't walk, to the nearest home goods store. We use ours every day for breakfast, lunch, or dinner and sometimes all three. We might make bacon or hash browns for breakfast, a piece of salmon to go with a salad at lunch, and a whole chicken or steak for dinner. The appliance is faster than a conventional oven, easy to use, cleans up fast, and is able to fry without using any oil.

Food scale. If you are meal prepping for the week ahead, a food scale can be invaluable for making sure your meals are properly proportioned. They also come in handy when you are working with a recipe that lists the ingredients in grams or ounces. If you are serious about cooking and nutrition, a food scale can be a powerful ally.

chapter twenty

HOME FOR THE HOLIDAYS

Cameron

Our first Christmas together came just a month after our wedding in 2018. Lauren and I decided to celebrate in Maine. The Hamiltons do *not* hold back when it comes to holidays, so I was excited to show Lauren all our traditions.

We flew into town a couple days before Christmas. As we pulled up the driveway, the house was decked out in lights, holly, and a fresh layer of snow. Inside, Lauren admired all the wooden Santas scattered throughout the house. She first picked up the smallest Santa, about the size of a LEGO figure and wearing skis, which Mom had set on a windowsill that year at the front of the house. Lauren then moved on to the largest: a three-foot-tall stoic Santa standing guard in the front hall.

"Where did you get these?" she asked.

"Dad carved them and my aunt painted them," I explained.

"What? That's amazing!"

I was happy Lauren was already appreciating our traditions and I could not wait to show her one of the biggest of them all: the treasure hunt.

The tradition started when we were kids. For my sixth birthday, my parents came up with an elaborate treasure hunt involving a parchment paper map with singed edges and a wooden chest with skull and crossbones, all handmade. They created a bunch of cryptic clues that took us all around the house and yard. The tradition has evolved so that treasure hunts now take place on family holidays like Easter, Thanksgiving, and especially Christmas. When we were kids, the prizes were chocolate coins and action figures. As my sister and I got older, the booty turned into little bottles of champagne, fireworks, and scratch-off tickets. The hunts have grown more elaborate as well.

It's become a sacred event for the family. So I was happy when Lauren dove in headfirst. In one leg of the hunt, we had to shoot a clay target to release the clue inside. Lauren took aim and nailed the target, even though it was her first time firing a gun.

"You're a natural," I said with a smile.

"Thanks, that was fun!" she replied, while pulling her jacket tighter around her.

After finding the treasure, we went back inside and had some tea to warm up from the frigid expedition. I began divvying up the loot to everyone, including the scratch-off tickets.

"Here you go, scratch away," I said, passing Lauren a ticket. As I began working on my own, I heard Lauren softly ask, "Cameron, is this right?"

Lauren handed me her ticket. I looked it up and down several times, hardly believing what I was seeing.

"Yes, it is," I said.

"I won five thousand dollars!" she cried.

Lauren

Winning those five G's was definitely a shock. As Cameron and family took turns checking out the ticket, I thought to myself, *This is a sign that I'm where I'm supposed to be.* The whole experience of Christmas in Maine was really, really special. But Cam is right: his family does not mess around with the traditions. The morning we arrived, I was met with a twelve-foot spruce that Cam's dad, Poppa Hamilton, had cut down himself. On Christmas morning, the presents were literally overflowing from the living room into the dining room.

Christmas in the Speed household was a little different, though we always celebrated as a family. Relatives would come in from all over for a few days of singing, laughing, and cooking. My dad would put on Marvin Gaye or some holiday soul music. We'd sing along with the classics, dance to our favorites, and drink our holiday cocktails (spiced *and* spiked for the grown-ups!). Later, we'd pile into the family room to watch old family videos and flip through photo albums.

Now that Cam and I are creating our own holidays, we're drawing on the best of our family traditions. For our first Thanksgiving together, we had everyone to our home in Atlanta. I was so nervous in the days before about hosting for the first time. I wanted the food to be perfect and for everyone to get along and have a good time. I think a lot of holiday stress comes from all the high expectations. But as soon as everyone settled in, with the moms in the kitchen cooking and the dads out on the front porch drinking beer, I remembered the true meaning of the holiday.

Later, we sat down to an insane feast. My mom had worked her magic with the turkey. Cam's mom made the apple pies. My dad was on sides detail, including greens and yams. And I made my signature mac 'n' cheese. As we took our seats at the table, my brother spoke up. He had been quiet throughout the day, so I was pleasantly surprised by his participation.

"I'd like to give the Thanksgiving prayer," he said. He then proceeded to deliver the most beautiful and profound prayer. It was like something out of a movie.

Cameron

It's been such a joy finding our holiday spirit together, and that includes matters of faith and religion. While I have always had my own spirituality, the way that Lauren has come into my life has strengthened my convictions. As with all the most important topics, we started this discussion back in the pods.

"Tell me about your spirituality," I asked Lauren.

"I have traditional Christian beliefs," Lauren answered, "but I also have my own take on it. So while I don't necessarily go to church every Sunday, prayer is an important part of my life, and I try to listen to sermons regularly online. I have a strong connection to God, and I like to keep it on my own terms."

"I can relate to that," I said, explaining that I grew up in a Christian household and that I was confirmed into the Church. I also detailed how I spent a large part of my adolescence and

Lauren's Mac 'n' Cheese

Ingredients
1 lb elbow macaroni pasta
Olive oil
4 tbsp unsalted butter
1 ½ cups half-and-half
1 cup 2% milk
2 tbsps all-purpose flour
4 oz mascarpone cheese (cream cheese works too)
8 oz Muenster cheese, shredded
8 oz Monterey Jack cheese, shredded
8 oz sharp cheddar cheese, shredded
4 oz Colby Jack cheese, shredded
1 tsp salt
1 tsp onion powder
1 tsp garlic powder
1 tsp smoked paprika
1 tsp cayenne pepper (optional)
½ tsp black pepper

Instructions
1. Preheat the oven to 350°F.

2. Bring a pot of water to a boil, then add in the pasta.

3. Cook the pasta until it is al dente, then drain the water and lightly toss in olive oil.

4. In a large sauce pan, melt the butter over medium-low heat.

5. Add flour to the melted butter and whisk until smooth.

6. Add milk and half-and-half to the mixture and whisk in slowly.

7. Reduce the heat to low, then add the cheese, reserving some for topping. Stir continuously.

8. Add in salt, onion powder, garlic powder, paprika, cayenne (if using), and black pepper and continue to stir until the cheese sauce is smooth.

9. Transfer the pasta into a 9 x 13-inch baking dish, then pour the cheese sauce over the pasta and mix.

10. Spread the reserved cheese on top until fully covered.

11. Bake for 25 to 30 minutes.

12. Remove from the oven and let cool for 5 to 10 minutes.

Bon appétit!

adulthood studying world religions and trying to reconcile my religion and philosophy research with my science-based understanding of the world.

"What are your beliefs?" Lauren asked.

"I have many beliefs, but the guiding one is that having compassion for one's self and others leads to a higher connection to God," I said. "That's why I believe Christianity has tremendous merit. Jesus Christ is such a positive role model, in the way that he preached universal love and the golden rule of doing unto others as you would have done unto yourself. I think practicing compassion is the one thing we can all agree leads to a better world."

"How do you feel about going to church with me or praying with me?" Lauren asked.

"I am happy to pray with you or listen to a sermon with you. I support you in your pursuit of prayer and connection to God." Even though Lauren and I do not have identical beliefs, we are still able to strengthen our spiritual connection with each other through shared prayer and recognition of how God put us together to bring more good into the world.

When this topic comes up with regards to children, it's with the same spirit of compassion and tolerance. I have no problem with our kids going to church or learning the teachings of Christianity, as long as they understand that they will ultimately get to make their own decisions.

Lauren

I do want to raise our children in the Church, but really I want to raise good people who respect others and the world. Cameron and I share that larger value, so I know we'll always find the right compromise when it comes to our family's spirituality and religion.

Sometimes I dream about a big house, fully decked out, Hamilton-style, with lights and candles in every room and a big ol' Christmas tree in the corner. Both families are there—parents, siblings, and other relatives, including my aunt Sheila, who is grooving out with her old-school dance moves to some Motown Christmas album, like the Temptations or Diana Ross. Out back, Sparx is rolling around with his pooch pal, one of the latest additions to the family. Then there's the very best part of the fantasy— our pride and joy, baby Hamilton. I don't know if it's a boy or girl, and it doesn't matter. All I pray for is continued blessings for our entire family. Together with the love Cameron and I share, the celebration of family is our highest virtue of all. And the holidays are special to us.

Avoiding a Holiday Train Wreck

The holidays are all about comfort and joy. But let's face it, they can also be incredibly stressful. All the time spent together creates a lot of opportunities for conflict. Here are a few rules for steering clear of strife and holiday burnout:

Practice tolerance. If you're spending the holidays at the in-laws', recognize that they will have some traditions that are different from your own. Try to be open to the new experiences. Who knows—you may experience something like a new food or activity that makes the holiday even more special for you.

Manage expectations. There's no such thing as a perfect holiday. Don't be discouraged if the festivities don't turn out exactly as you planned. Likewise, if you're hosting for the first time, don't put too much pressure on yourself to create the *Best. Holiday. Ever.* The most important thing is that you are getting together with the people that you love and appreciating the nature of the holiday. Everything else is just extra.

Keep it simple. The most memorable holiday moments are often simple ones—trimming the tree or taking a family walk before Thanksgiving dinner. It's worth taking a moment to look around and take a mental snapshot. It is a blessing to have people you love in your life.

chapter twenty-one

SUDDEN CELEBRITY

Cameron

The whole time Lauren and I were starting a life together, we knew that another narrative about our relationship was taking shape in the editing room of *Love Is Blind*. We reached out to Production many times before the show premiered, asking for any kind of update. Each time we called, they assured us they were working very hard on the edits, but that they didn't want to commit to a release date yet because there was still work to do. After the calls, Lauren and I would break down what was discussed to determine if there were any clues in what Production had told us. After a year of anxiously waiting, we finally got word of the premiere date, but we didn't get any kind of sneak peek. We had to watch the February 13, 2020, premiere on Netflix just like everyone else.

Lauren

After nearly a year and a half of waiting, you can imagine how anxious we were. We were at home in Atlanta at the time. The show actually premiered at 3:00 a.m. EST, but we ultimately decided it was best to get some rest, since we had no idea what to expect once the show was out there in the world. We woke up around 6:00 a.m., made some coffee and tea, and settled in to watch what we'd been waiting for what felt like a lifetime. Once we began watching, it was like being transported back to those moments in time; we were taken back to the pods. The emotions rushed back when we watched ourselves walking into the facility for the first time and having our first pod date.

Later that week, we went to Krog Street Market, a popular Millennial hangout in Atlanta. We were grabbing some food when all of a sudden a group of people came up to us. "It's so great to see you guys together," one of them said. We smiled and said polite thank-yous but then got out of there as quickly as we could. That was the last time we went out anywhere busy until the official press tour a couple weeks later.

Cameron

For nearly a year and a half, Lauren and I had been living a quiet married life. There was solace in our anonymity—few people knew about Lauren's and my journey together, so we were free to grow our relationship without outside opinions weighing in. We had been careful not to post each other on social media, even though we were excited to share our relationship. All of that changed with the premiere of the show. Now people were commenting every minute of every day on our posts, letting us know what they thought of us and our relationship. And so with the premiere of *Love Is Blind*, we found the start of another test for our marriage: learning how to block out the opinions of others.

The day Lauren and I were shown to our courtside seats at Madison Square Garden, a few minutes before tip-off to the Knicks game, was the day our newfound fame truly started to sink in. It was the first week in March 2020 and we were in New York City for the *LIB* press tour, which had premiered a few weeks earlier. For Lauren and me, it felt like our first time stepping out into the public eye, so there was no margin for error: we hired a wardrobe stylist, a hair stylist, and a makeup artist—the whole nine yards. It was all very different from the show, which required us to do all that ourselves.

We were looking and feeling our best for our Big Apple debut. The day had been a whirlwind of new experiences, from our first paparazzi encounter with the well-known celebrity photographer Miles Diggs (aka Diggzy) to interviews on huge platforms such as the *Today* show, PeopleTV, and Barstool Sports. Our publicist made sure we hit every possible media outlet we could that day and in the days that followed. By the time we made it to the game, we were coasting on fumes, but we weren't about to miss an opportunity to sit courtside at Madison Square Garden. It was a trip to look around and see celebrities—we even spotted the rapper Cam'ron making his way to a nearby seat. During halftime, I headed to the lounge MSG had generously provided us access to and ran into Cam'ron in the bathroom. "Nice suit," he said as he passed by.

I made it back to my seat beside Lauren just as the Celebrity Cam took over the Jumbotron that hung from the rafters, high above center court. All of a sudden, there he was again.

"That's crazy; I just ran into him in the bathroom," I said to Lauren. "He complimented my suit."

"Isn't this amazing?" said Lauren when suddenly the Celebrity Cam panned to us.

"From the runaway hit Netflix show *Love Is Blind*, it's Lauren and Cameron Hamilton!" the loudspeaker blared. The crowd went wild. Then they played a clip from the show, the toothbrush scene (of course!). The Garden crew had slipped us a couple brushes, so we improvised a little skit where we pretended to brush each other's teeth. The crowd went wild.

"It's hard to believe that everyone knows us here," I said, staring up at the full-capacity crowd. If there was any doubt about our sudden celebrity, the chants of "Lauren and Cameron" wiped it away.

Lauren

The speed with which it all happened was truly incredible. I remember the Jumbotron moment, but for me it was the Shonda Rhimes tweet that made it real. She was a huge role model of mine, given her massive success as a Black author and TV producer. A couple weeks into *Love Is Blind*, I was scrolling through Twitter when I noticed a tweet from her. "I'm obsessed with Cameron and Lauren," she wrote. My head just about exploded.

A few days later, Trevor Noah mentioned us on *The Daily Show*.

"Oh my God!" I shouted. "Trevor Noah knows who we are!"

Then came the ultimate moment of arrival for any cultural phenomenon: the *Saturday Night Live* spoof. This is something Cameron and I had joked about previously.

"What if the show becomes so big that it gets the *SNL* treatment?" I asked him during one of our dates. We imagined who would play us. Ego Nwodim for me? Mikey Day for Cameron?

As it turned out, the skit didn't parody actual cast members from *Love Is Blind*. But there were some pretty obvious references—right down to my exact hoop earrings from the show (it was Nwodim who played a knock-off of me, a "picture taker" named Raquel). And to be honest, it was hilarious.

The *SNL* skit introduced us to the darker side of celebrity, where you become the joke, the punchline, one I was aware of going into *Love Is Blind*. I wouldn't say I dreaded it, but I knew I had to proceed with caution, keeping my wits about me and not jumping in headfirst. Because my dad worked in the industry, he taught me from an early age that fame can be really ugly. Even though I fantasized about being a performer as a kid—I loved the performing arts and worked hard toward being the best I could be in the different veins of creatively expressing myself—I always knew it wasn't for the thin-skinned or faint of heart.

Cameron

I didn't have the same exposure to stardom's seedier side as a kid, but I came into *Love Is Blind* prepared. My mind-set was always, *If I'm going to do this, I'm going to keep an open mind and I'm going to give it 100 percent. I'm not here to ham it up for the camera.* I wanted people to see me for who I really am, whether it was the women on the other side of the wall or the people who would later watch at home.

In the facility, I got the sense that not everyone was being their authentic selves. I've talked about how quickly cast members would switch into their representative selves anytime the camera panned their way. While I think we were all intrigued by the notion of being on television, many seemed more focused on the notoriety they could gain than the possibility of finding love. I chuckled when one guy whispered to me, "Bro, we're gonna be famous after this." I didn't have the heart to tell him the microphone could still pick up his audio.

The interesting thing is, most of the people who did not seem focused on forming connections were among the first wave of departures from the show. I think both the cast and Production quickly got a sense of who was open to forming a connection and who had ulterior motives.

Lauren

The star-chasing got pretty bad on the girls' side of *Love Is Blind* too. One morning a couple of the ladies were having some drinks, mixing up a couple of Bloody Marys.

"Can you guys imagine if this show blows up?" one of them said.

"Totally," the other responded. "I heard that anyone who gets married will have their own spread in *People*."

"No way, *People* magazine!" a third gal chimed in, sidling up to the bar. "We could be famous!"

Like Cameron said, these were the first people to get shown the door, which is ironic.

Of course, Cam and I were aware of the possibility of celebrity. But we tried not to focus on it too much. For one thing, we didn't want to be too disappointed if the show flopped. How humiliating would that be, to go around town bragging and boasting and then watch the show crash out at the bottom of the ratings? So our motto was always "Don't get too excited."

Then there was the dark side of stardom, the vulnerability to criticism and mockery, that I mentioned earlier. A big part of it stems from the fact that when you're in the public eye you're no longer in control of your own story. That's doubly true for reality television, where producers and editors determine the narrative for you. The audience, in turn, feels like they've followed your story from the beginning. They feel like they're right there with you. That's beautiful in a way. And I do look at our supporters as our extended family. But at the same time, it can be tough when some of them feel entitled to tell you how to live your life moving forward.

That's where trolling comes in. I remember I did an Instagram Live one time, you know, being myself, with my big personality. But some of the viewers couldn't handle it.

"Who is this person?" one of them wrote. "This is not the same Lauren from the show. She's so loud and ghetto."

"You've really changed, Lauren," another follower commented.

It was hard to read those comments, because I'm the same person I've always been. On *Love Is Blind*, I was genuinely looking for love, so of course I was going to show a softer side. And like most of the cast, the rawness of the emotions had me feeling vulnerable and exposed, so that part of my personality came through the most. But the fun boisterous side was always there.

Here's the thing, though: for every negative comment, there were a hundred positive ones. We have people from all over the world sending messages about how our story changed their lives. So much love and support from my sisters, sharing things like: "It's so amazing to see another woman of color on TV like you, being herself and being loved. We love to see it."

Cameron

Fame truly is a double-edged sword. Lauren and I have experienced its invasive nature many times now, including at LAX on our way home from the LA leg of the *LIB* press tour. We were both wiped out from the days of back-to-back interviews and public appearances. We were sitting down at a restaurant near the terminal having a quick bite to eat.

I was about to enjoy my cheeseburger when this guy got right up in our faces and stood there staring, waiting for us to acknowledge him. Finally, he said, "You guys are from that TV show, right?"

I set the burger down and gave him a subtle nod. He then started to barrage us with questions: Was the show for real? Were we really married? How much did we get paid?

We did our best to be polite, but at a certain point I had to say to him, "Hey! I'm sorry, our flight is in a few minutes. Do you mind if we finish eating?"

We have had our share of unexpected encounters with fans of us and the show. The vast majority have been overwhelmingly positive: We have been given fan art that we've hung all around our house. We have been showered with gifts and opportunities beyond anything I could have ever expected or asked for going into the experiment. We have received thousands of messages from supporters telling us how our love story has inspired them to keep looking for their partner or to work on improving their own relationship. Knowing that Lauren's and my love for each other has helped bring more love into the lives of others makes all of the invasive and negative comments pale in comparison.

One of my favorite experiences from our NYC press tour was going on *Sway in the Morning*, a music and culture show on SiriusXM. I'd been a huge fan of Sway and his radio show since my college days. My friend Shashi, who produced and collaborated with me on our songs, and I would watch his show every week. Sway always had some of our favorite rappers, like Wiz Khalifa and Big Sean, on his show. They'd talk music and entertainment and then Sway would put on some instrumentals and get them to freestyle.

It was a surreal moment sitting in the studio with him. When the morning started, our publicist had told us we were doing several interviews at the SiriusXM HQ. I had not considered that we would be going on *Sway in the Morning*, much less thought about the possibility I would be asked to freestyle. Although I wish I had more forewarning, the surprise of it all saved me from the anxiety I would have felt getting ready for it. As fate would have it, Sway played the same beat for me that he had Wiz rap over all those years ago. All in all, performing on Sway's show was electrifying and I am honored I got that opportunity. Plus, my parents said it was their favorite interview, because they recognized Sway is a genuine man and they felt Lauren and I had the best energy talking with him. They weren't wrong!

After the show, Sway took Lauren and me aside and offered us some fatherly advice. "This industry will seduce you," he said. "You have to make a concerted effort to not lose track of what's meaningful to you guys. Stay true to yourselves, to each other, and to your families, and the rest will take care of itself."

chapter twenty-two

SCROLLING RIGHT ALONG

Lauren

Social media is both heaven and hell. On the one hand, it's been the best way for Cam and me to tell the story of our marriage, beyond the interracial dating narrative that was created for us on *Love Is Blind*. We love being able to talk directly to our fans and supporters and let them into our lives on a more intimate level. That's the positive. On the other hand, it means we're constantly under the microscope and, as a result, subject to constant scrutiny and criticism.

As we've said before, most of the comments we get online, whether via Instagram, TikTok, YouTube, or some other social media platform, are filled with love and support. But there's always a small sliver of the audience that feels the need to weigh in with advice.

If I post a video from one of my fitness workouts, someone will tell me how my technique is all wrong. Or if it's a share about my hair, I'll get all these suggestions about other looks to try. "Don't do it like that," they'll say. Or maybe: "Why are you trying to change who you are?"

Poor Cam shared a video once about a gate he built in the yard. My man knows his way around a toolbox, so it came out great. But you wouldn't believe the deluge of comments: "That's the wrong size screw." "The hinge looks crooked." "Why did you choose *that* color?"

We appreciate the interest. Really, we do. But the constant feedback has definitely taken some getting used to.

Cameron

The adjustment to social media was difficult for me. Before *Love Is Blind*, I had a couple hundred followers on Instagram. I'd post once a month, at most. To be honest, I had always thought social media was a little vain. My attitude was basically, *What is the point of posting all these pictures of myself? What's the point of anyone posting pictures of themselves? Why even bother?* I told Lauren about my disinterest in social media, but slowly she changed my perspective. "Social media is more important than you realize," she said. "People want to connect with who they see on TV. This is your chance to talk to those people and share your thoughts with them."

During the shooting of *Love Is Blind*, we didn't have our phones, so that was a complete social media blackout. I appreciated that, because it meant Lauren and I could really focus on each other and on our burgeoning love.

Cut to early 2020, a month before the February 13 premiere. After Lauren's and my discussions, I had started posting more regularly in anticipation of the show coming out. Meanwhile, Netflix started to run trailers for the show, along with other social media assets. They were looking to tease the show and get some buzz going online. It was a strange sensation to watch the followers start trickling in. I was both excited to see people were already anticipating the show and anxious for what was to come. Even though I wasn't part of the pre-show press—Lauren and Mark were the faces of the show at that time—I reached one thousand followers before my name was even released to the media. I was impressed with how resourceful people were in finding me from a trailer on YouTube.

On February 10, Netflix released another clip from the show online. The snippet was from one of Lauren's and my first dates in the pods. The response was overwhelming. Once the first episode of *Love Is Blind* was released, tens of thousands of new followers started pouring in every day, all with something to say. During our NYC press tour, I remember seeing over a hundred thousand new followers in a single day. I did not want to get caught up in focusing on followers and likes, but when hundreds of thousands of people are engaged with what you say and do online, it is difficult to ignore. At the time of writing this book, I was just short of 2 million followers on Instagram—closing in on Lauren's 2.5 million! Not that it's a competition, of course.

As our audience continued to grow, I started to understand the appeal of social media. Our supporters had become invested in our love story and I began to feel an obligation to keep them up to date on our daily adventures. Though the most devoted supporters, however, had little trouble keeping up with us on their own, usually through some pretty sophisticated sleuthing on social media.

For example, when the show first started streaming on Netflix in February 2020, many wanted to figure out if we eventually made it to the altar and were still together. These internet Sherlocks found clues everywhere! They matched the faint reflection of Lauren in my sunglasses in one of my pictures to a photo of Lauren on her own Instagram account. They also cross-examined a picture of our Christmas tree that Lauren posted in 2018 to one that Mom posted in 2019 and matched the ornaments between pictures. The internet does not like to be surprised.

While we were going through *Love Is Blind*, I was solely focused on strengthening my relationship with Lauren. When I started connecting with our supporters, I saw that our story had inspired others not to give up hope for their own love life. And our support does not just come from the US but from all over the world and from all different demographics. Some of the largest sections of our audience come from Canada, the UK, Germany, Brazil, South Africa, and Australia. We have been truly blessed to have the opportunity to inspire others all around the world to keep hope alive and find their love.

Lauren

Oh my God, I've created a monster! Lol. Despite the good and bad of social media, I think Cameron and I have found a happy medium. The trick is to be transparent while still maintaining some sense of mystery. I want to be relatable online, so I don't just show the highlights from my life. It's a mistake to present a too polished version of yourself online. That's why I'll also occasionally post my natural self. Makeup-less, weave-less, and without a filter to normalize looking like your natural beautiful self. I don't want people to get this perfect perception of me, because I'm not perfect. I want my supporters to know that I'm a human being.

That being said, there is such a thing as oversharing, especially when it comes to romance. When I was a little girl, my aunt always gave me the best relationship advice: If you and your mate have a disagreement, she said, keep it behind closed doors. But as soon as you go outside, you need to have a united front. Discuss problems in the home, not the streets.

I've taken my aunt's words to heart, especially when it comes to social media. Cameron and I have our disagreements, just like my aunt promised we would. But that's not something I would ever talk about on social media. It wouldn't benefit anyone, and it would only open us up to an avalanche of unwanted advice and criticism.

Cameron

As Lauren said, social media is all about balance. That's a big reason why we launched the *Hanging with the Hamiltons* channel on YouTube. It's been a way to let our supporters into our lives on a deeper level while telling the stories we want to tell.

In between our NYC and LA press tours, we cooked up a name for the channel, recorded the goofy title song, collaborated on a loose script for the welcome video, and then sat down on the couch in our living room and hit the record button.

We posted the video on March 7, a couple days after the premiere of the *LIB* reunion show, when the buzz was reaching a crescendo and people were hungry for more information about us. Even after I saw my Instagram followers explode, it was amazing to see the number of views tick up on YouTube, from thousands to tens of thousands to millions.

A couple weeks later, we posted our second video, a Q&A based on questions from our Instagram supporters, and it made it onto the YouTube Trending page. That was crazy, especially for a new channel. It's one thing to trend if you're established with a built-in audience. But it happened for us straight out of the gate. We knew we were on to something.

Lauren

It's been quite a ride, and it's far from over. I love that Cameron and I are creative partners in addition to life partners. Not that we don't butt heads. I sometimes have to check myself, because, you know, content is my thing. I've been creating it for the better part of twenty years.

One time we were setting up a shoot in the house. Cam wanted to set the camera up on one side of the room.

"Let's move the camera over here," I said.

"Why can't we shoot from here?" he asked.

"Because it will look better in this frame," I answered.

"Why?" he asked.

"Because the lighting is better!" I snapped. "The background is better! It's just better!!" Then I added, "You know, you didn't give this much sass to the producers on the show. You have to think of me like that. If we were building an AI computer, I wouldn't tell you what to do!"

"Okay, okay, I was just asking," he said.

Working together is part of our relationship now. It's another way we're coming together as a couple.

And as with all things social media, we always try to keep in mind that they're only apps. Real life is always going to be more important than anything online. I don't care how popular the platform is, it could disappear at any moment. Then what? If you're experiencing your entire life through an app, what will you be left with? That's the question you always have to ask yourself.

Fave Moments on Social Media

Social media is all about engagement. It is about creating content that people can relate to and have something to say about. That's why we're always looking for fun, new ways to interact with our supporters. Here are a few of our favorite moments:

Wedding watch parties. This memory dates back to the *LIB* wedding-day finale in March 2020. In the days leading up, we noticed that many of our fans were talking about what *they* were going to wear for our big day. As it turned out, fans all over the world hosted wedding watch parties. Some even printed out life-size pictures of our faces and used them as masks. And there were a lot of cakes and cupcakes with our likenesses printed on them. We were so thankful to see how invested supporters were in our love story and how it gave them hope that they could go out and find a similar love of their own.

TikTok dances. After finishing the NYC and LA press tours, we found ourselves quarantined at home, still reeling from the excitement of the last few weeks. So like the rest of the world trying to figure out where to channel that pent-up energy, we turned to TikTok. Once our dance to Cookiee Kawaii's song "Vibe" went viral, we were hooked! Some of our favorites include reenacting the *Titanic* end scene, our clothing roulette wheel, being my wife for a day, and our many dance routines. We learned that sometimes the simplest Tik-Toks make the biggest waves: our video of Cameron spontaneously dancing to Saweetie's "My Type" has more than 14 million views.

Quarantine Diaries. As with TikTok, we wanted to make the most out of being in quarantine. After a few brainstorming sessions we realized what better way to do that than by creating a mockumentary about our experience in quarantine we called *The Quarantine Diaries*. The series really took off, and we think the reason for that is because it features situations we can all relate to during quarantine: work getting interrupted by home life, coming up with ways to entertain while being stuck inside, and being driven crazy by your spouse and your pets. The best part of *The Quarantine Diaries* was the chance we got to work together to create comedy, which is something we both cherish.

Lauren's Jeep surprise. Lauren has dreamed of having a white Jeep Wrangler since watching *Clueless* as a young girl. For her, it is more than a vehicle—it is a symbol of independence and adventure. When Cameron learned of what it meant to Lauren, he came up with a plan to surprise her with the Jeep and record her reaction for a YouTube video. It was incredibly rewarding, as Lauren got her childhood dream fulfilled and Cameron got to make that happen and capture her joy.

chapter twenty-three

NEW REALITIES

Cameron

So what's next? Lauren and I ask ourselves that question all the time. We're grateful to have supporters who let us know they also want to see where we're headed. When we asked our community what questions we should answer in The Newlywed Game on an episode of *Hanging with the Hamiltons*, the biggest question on everyone's mind was "When are y'all having a baby?" However, the runner-up question was "Where do I see us in ten years?"

"Business owners with kids in their dream home living happily," Lauren wrote on her whiteboard. My response: "Two kids, we have a business together, I have my separate AI business, a big house for our whole family, and two dogs." (Not bad for a former dog-a-phobe!)

Lauren's and my journey together is just beginning. Ambition is one of the things we first connected over back in the pods, and our vision and goals have only increased since then. We want to build an empire together and we're not afraid to admit it, in the same way we've never shied away from showing vulnerability in our relationship.

Lauren and I want to continue creating together in much the same way. There are so many more stories we want to tell. To that end, we acquired the studio space we've been dreaming of and assembled a production team so that we can make content on a larger scale. On our YouTube channel, we are focusing on the story of our marriage and our family as it continues to grow. We also have our show, *The Love Seat*, where we dig into everything from love languages to long-distance relationships to keeping the romance going in marriage. We're also continuing to develop scripted narratives that give us a chance to tell stories that extend beyond us and our lives. Lauren and I love sharing our narratives and connecting with people, so we're excited to see where that passion leads us in the years to come.

Lauren

Empires aren't built in a day. We know that. That's why we make sure to have short-term goals in addition to the longer-term ones. Even if you're not actually running a business with your spouse the way Cameron and I are, it's important to run your marriage like a business. You can do that and still have time for fun and romance. In fact, the more seriously you take the logistics of marriage, the more time and energy you'll have for pleasurable pursuits. Remember, it's all about finding balance. Organization is key to that.

In our weekly Monday planning meetings, we'll often use mock seriousness to keep it light. "Thank you for attending today's meeting, Mr. Hamilton," I might say. "On the agenda for today is X, Y, and Z." We'll cover any content deadlines that are happening that week or new branding opportunities to discuss. And we'll cover personal commitments, from doctors' visits to plans with friends and family. Having a firm handle on the short-term itinerary frees up the time and mental energy needed for more ambitious long-term planning.

Cameron

Family looms large in our long-term planning. We have settled on the idea of two kids (three on accident as Lauren likes to say), though we obviously recognize that we don't have total control over the miracle of life. Whatever happens, we will accept the blessing.

We do have some control over the timing. More and more, I envision myself as a father: reading books to the kids until they fall asleep, kicking a soccer ball around with them in the backyard, teaching them how to help out around the house. I recognize becoming a father will come with trying days and continuous work, but I also think about how much I appreciate everything my parents did. My deep admiration for my parents inspires me to want to raise children with Lauren and watch them grow into their own people.

On the other side, Lauren and I celebrated our two-year anniversary in November 2020 and still enjoy focusing on each other. Of course, we understand that couples continue evolving together, kids or not, but we also know children are a massive commitment in all respects. We are still tuning the dynamics of our working relationship and are relishing this opportunity we have to create together. If it looks effortless, then we are doing our job, because the truth is that what we create requires a constant, concerted effort. Sharing our lives with the world is truly rewarding for us, so we wouldn't have it any other way. But when we bring a baby into the world, we want to make sure we have our work lives as managed as possible so we can devote our energy to our child.

Lauren and I also have other items left on our pre-kids checklist, including travel. We have support from all around the world, including Brazil, Germany, South Africa, Australia, Japan, and many more places. We would love to visit these countries and get to know the people and culture of each. We also have visions of owning a larger home all four of our parents can stay in periodically and help raise our children.

Lauren

That's not what people want to hear, we know. Especially my mother!

"What do you mean 'a few years'?" she asked the last time we talked about it. "I'm ready for grandkids right now!"

"You know that's not how it works, right?" I teased.

She has plenty of support from our fans. Like we've said, they are constantly looking for any sign that I'm carrying.

"Check out the glow on Lauren's face," one commenter wrote recently. "Oh she's definitely pregnant!"

"Her face looks fuller," another added. "It must be on."

I'm like, "Um, no, my face is fuller because we've been quarantined and I've been eating potato chips for breakfast!"

Seriously, though, the pandemic has loomed large through the early phase of our marriage—remember, it first struck the US right around the time of the February 2020 *LIB* premiere. Being in quarantine has forced us to confront issues head-on, including how to share space and how to make time apart, even when you're together 24/7. It's also given us a better understanding of what it means to be a stand-up partner. When you're in lockdown, small disagreements can quickly snowball into major issues. It's fortunate that our relationship started from a place of compassion and communication in the pods (which, when you think about it, were a kind of quarantine). During the pandemic, we've been able to use those tools to practice patience with each other and take each day as it comes.

That goes for family planning too. Cam and I are used to the pregnancy pressure by now. We're happy to keep everyone in suspense. And that's the advice we give other couples. When it comes to starting a family, the only timeline that matters is the one you and your partner agree to.

Cameron

From the beginning of our relationship, the focus has been on each other, without letting outside voices interfere. From producers trying to nudge us in one direction or another, to family and friends weighing in, to supporters and critics all over the world telling us what they think of our relationship—the key is to block out outside influence and concentrate on doing what we agree is right for us and our relationship. This means many different things: never talking behind each other's back, respecting each other's individuality and need for space, not keeping secrets, continuing to have conversations about things that bother us, and so much more. We don't always get it right, but our relationship continues to grow each day.

I think back to our very first date in the pods. When I talked about "taking over the world" to Lauren, I meant through my work in AI. I had everything mapped out in my mind and planned on going it alone. People routinely ask me, "Are you still a scientist? Do you still work in AI?" The simple answer is that I will always be a scientist; it is part of who I am. Instead of working for a corporation, I now operate my own business, Alliance AI, where I only work on projects I am passionate about. One of my passion projects is a virtual assistant aimed at helping people with memory disorders. The biggest challenge for me now is balancing my AI projects with the creative projects Lauren and I collaborate on. However, it's a good problem to have—I wouldn't have it any other way. Put simply, my work in AI is still a critical part of the plan, and my relationship with Lauren has only added to my vision for the future.

What I've come to realize is that a relationship does not fix the problems in your life: you yourself are responsible for becoming whole. A truly satisfying relationship is one where you both retain your individuality while simultaneously enriching each other's life through mutual love, respect, and compassion. A love like that is the most empowering force in the world. With Lauren by my side, there's nothing we can't do.

Lauren

It reminds me of something I said after our first pod date: "I'm ready to continue with this experiment." I was referring to the *LIB* experiment. But what *I've* come to understand is that love itself is the actual experiment. When Cameron and I committed to a life together, it was the ultimate leap of faith. Saying "I do" wasn't the end of the experiment. It was just the beginning. The future is filled with unknowns. And love is most definitely blind. But with true love on our side, Cameron and I can see everything so much more clearly.

acknowledgments

We would first like to thank our family at CAA, particularly Cindy Uh and Kate Childs, for guiding us through every step of the process. We are grateful to Simon & Schuster/Gallery Books for believing in our story and taking such great care of us. In particular, we would like to thank Natasha Simons and Maggie Loughran for providing crucial feedback on every draft of this book, as well as Jennifer Robinson, Lisa Litwack, and Abby Zidle. We would also like to thank Dan DiClerico and Rebecca Paley for their invaluable input in telling our story. We are grateful to Momma Hamilton for providing feedback on the later drafts as well. We are so appreciative of the unwavering support our friends and family have shown us throughout this entire process—including when we got married on a TV show! Last, but definitely not least, we would like to thank our supporters for your constant love and for inspiring us to write this book. You all are the best of the best.